D0711169

Pneumatic Correctives

What is the Spirit Saying to the Church of the 21st Century?

Michael J. Tkacik
Thomas C. McGonigle, O.P.

UNIVERSITY PRESS OF AMERICA,® INC.
Lanham • Boulder • New York • Toronto • Plymouth, UK

Copyright © 2007 by
University Press of America,® Inc.
4501 Forbes Boulevard
Suite 200
Lanham, Maryland 20706
UPA Acquisitions Department (301) 459-3366

Estover Road
Plymouth PL6 7PY
United Kingdom

Library of Congress Control Number: 2006934499
ISBN-13: 978-0-7618-3569-1 (paperback : alk. paper)
ISBN-10: 0-7618-3569-5 (paperback : alk. paper)

This book is dedicated

To our Mothers, Anne Elizabeth and Elva,

Who lovingly taught us

To be faithful to our friends

To speak the truth

And to walk in service to the People of God

Acknowledgments

Tom and I would like to acknowledge all those who encouraged and supported us as we discussed and worked on this book, particularly our colleagues and students, especially those who read portions of the manuscript and offered feedback and suggestions. A special thanks is owed to Shelley Douglas for her detailed editing of the manuscript. I also want to recognize my family for all of the love and support that they give me as I strive to live in fidelity to the prompting of the Spirit, especially my Dad for his guidance and wisdom, and Suzy who showers me with *kenotic* and *agapic* love. Lastly, for my sons, Charles Joseph, Benjamin David and Samuel Nathan, Father Tom and I hope and pray that the Church of the future—your Church—is one that is life-giving to you, affirms your charisms and baptismal dignity, is marked by servant-leadership, and, above all, is faithful to what the Spirit is saying.

Michael J. Tkacik
Saint Leo University
Saint Leo, Florida
Summer 2006

Introduction

THE CHURCH: THE SACRAMENT OF THE PASCHAL MYSTERY TO THE WORLD

Lumen Gentium, Vatican II's Dogmatic Constitution on the Church, articulates a vision of the Church inspired by the Holy Spirit in response to the "signs of the times" calling the Church of the 21st century to become anew the People of God journeying together in history to become the Sacrament of the Paschal Mystery for the world. By identifying the Church as the sacrament of Christ to the world, the Council mandates that the Church must point to and make present Christ to the world. This task is universal in scope, for Jesus came to save all people, and the Council commits the Church to the perpetuation of Christ's selfsame mission—the salvation of all (See *Lumen Gentium* #'s 9, 13, 16,17 and *Gaudium et Spes* #'s 42 and 45). Furthermore, the bishops note that "the present conditions of the world add greater urgency to this work of the Church . . ."(*Lumen Gentium* #1). Such a vision demands that the Church respond to "the joys and hopes, the griefs and anxieties of people of this age" (*Gaudium et Spes* #1) in a manner that sheds light on how the life, death and resurrection of Jesus Christ provides meaning to the life experience of all persons. Additionally, the Church, herself, must embody and exemplify the *kenotic* (self-emptying) and *agapic* (unconditional) love of the One of whom she is a sacrament. Inculturation and fidelity to the Holy Spirit are key to the Church's sacramental mission.

To be successful in her efforts to proclaim and witness the meaning that Christ has for the world, the Church must surrender to the prompting and call of the Holy Spirit. This will require that the directives of renewal introduced at the Second Vatican Council be even more fully developed. As Yves Congar,

Congar described Vatican II's pneumatological vision as follows:

> One of the most important ways in which the Holy Spirit has been restored to
> the pneumatological ecclesiology of the Council was in the sphere of charisms.
> This meant that the Church is built up not only by institutional means but also
> by the infinite variety of the gifts that each person has the right and duty to use
> in the Church and in the world for the good of humankind and for the upbuild-
> ing of the Church . . . in the freedom of the Holy Spirit Who breathes where He
> wills . . . He makes the Gospel a contemporary reality and enables people today
> to understand the Word of God . . . It is also to the Spirit that the Council at-
> tributed the perpetual renewal that the Church has to undergo if it is to be faith-
> ful to its Lord . . .[4]

THE PARALLEL AND PARTING THEOLOGIES
OF THE SECOND VATICAN COUNCIL

The Second Vatican Council confronted the Church with the task of developing a theological vision that was capable of articulating the Church's relevancy to the world. Multiple pastoral developments were introduced at the
Council towards this end. A broader sense of ecclesial mission and a univer-
salism and openness facilitated ecumenism and greater lay roles in the
Church. The call for a new theological vision and the pastoral steps under-
taken by the Council, however, tended to be introduced devoid of any theological underpinning capable of interpreting, understanding and implementing the new ecclesial vision and directives. What one finds in the teachings of
the Council is a tension between two operative theologies utilized by the
Council fathers: Classical Essentialism and Historical-Existentialism. The
tensions between the two theologies, as well as the inconsistent and concur-
rent application of the two theologies, leave incomplete the ecclesial enter-
prise introduced at Vatican II.

ECCLESIAL OPENNESS TO CULTURE

In order to extend the Church's mission to the world, the Church had to enter
into human history and learn from it (*Lumen Gentium* #'s 9, 13, 17). Hence
the Council's openness to culture. Such an openness is imperative if the
Church is to address the world's needs and thus demonstrate Her relevancy in
and to the world. The task self-imposed upon the Church at Vatican II demanded that the Church present herself as capable of illuminating human experience in meaningful and life-giving ways. Positing an "intimate link" be-

tween the Church and the world, the Council fathers recognized that evangelization must interact with the world on the world's terms.

> The Church, living in various circumstances in the course of time, has used the discoveries of different cultures so that in her preaching she might spread and explain the message of Christ to all nations, that she might examine it and more deeply understand it, that she might give it better expression in liturgical celebration and in the varied life of the community of the faithful (*Gaudium et Spes* #58).

Here we see that the Council fathers recognized and acknowledged that the Church is subject to the varying historical epochs in which she finds herself; that the many cultures of the world contribute to and enhance her ability to preach, spread and explain the Gospel; and that they increase her own understanding of the Gospel and assist her in discerning ways in which to liturgically celebrate this understanding. Inherent in such an openness to culture is a recognition on behalf of the Church that "humanity comes to a true and full humanity only through culture" (*Gaudium et Spes* #53). In short, the Council Fathers noted that since the Church and culture are mutually interdependent, theology must respect the cultural and historical context in which it finds itself (See *Ad Gentes Divinitus* #'s 16 and 22):

> The recent studies and findings of science, history and philosophy raise new questions which effect life and which demand new theological investigations. Furthermore, theologians . . . are invited to seek continually for more suitable ways of communicating doctrine to the people of their times; for the deposit of faith or the truths are one thing and the manner in which they are enunciated . . . is another . . . In pastoral care, sufficient use must be made . . . of the findings of the secular sciences . . . so that the faithful may be brought to a more adequate and mature life of faith . . . Thus the knowledge of God is better manifested and the preaching of the Gospel becomes clearer to human intelligence and shows itself to be relevant to people's actual conditions of life (*Gaudium et Spes* #62).

So intimate is the link between the Church and culture(s), that the Council Fathers admonished the faithful to harmonize their religious duties with their secular duties (*Lumen Gentium* #36); rejected the notion that one's faith can be separated from one's social conduct (*Gaudium et Spes* #43); claimed that social progress reveals the glory of God (*Gaudium et Spes* #34); and maintained that the historical environments of the world are to be sources from which religious values are drawn (*Gaudium et Spes* #53). In short, what the Council highlighted was the fact that the Church and world were connected via a dialectic of mutual interdependence. The Council depicted this relationship

A Classicist world view of culture maintains that there is but one culture which is normative, universal and permanent. The values it embraces and the meanings it communicates are universal in claim and scope. It appeals to an abstract ideal and its concerns are unchanging; it attends to universals rather than particulars. It is informed by classical philosophy . . . and issues laws which are universally applicable and truths which are eternal. Circumstances of time and place are accidental . . . Humanity itself is a universal concept reflecting an unchanging reality . . . When a Classicist understanding of culture prevails, theology is looked upon as a permanent achievement.[9]

John O'Malley, S.J. notes that such a world view assumes that the Church is beyond change, i.e., beyond the influence of history. Reform efforts would be attempts at preserving the Church's substance, morals and doctrines. The Church, in the Classical view, is viewed primarily as a doctrinal society, and her doctrines are to be protected from change. Clearly such a world view is not a historical view, but a metaphysical view.[10] Over time the notion of providentialism came to be associated with this substantialistic world view, i.e., God was seen as the supreme guide of history so that all events of the past were seen as willed by God and, therefore, again, beyond change. This mentality only served to reinforce the immutable nature of the Classical world view, the Church and her teachings.[11] Fr. O'Malley writes:

Metaphysical thinking now combined with meta-historical thinking . . . The record of the past was viewed as a storehouse of *exempla* from which one drew prescriptive patterns of action which were directly transferable to the present situation.[12]

The Classical world view stands at odds with the vision of Vatican II which tended toward the Historical Existential world view marked by a vision of the Church that emphasized an openness to worldly cultures, a universal sense of mission, the task of *aggiornamento*, etc. Or, as T. O'Meara succinctly states, "the presumption of an eternal metaphysics, i.e., a perennial definition of Church, undermines its historical and eschatological nature."[13]

Vatican II recognized that it belonged to the Church's very essence to change, for it was the Church's responsibility to learn from the various cultural forms of history and to apply what she learns to her self renewal.[14] Lucien Richard, O.M.I. maintains that the Council fathers sensed:

That there is a new situation that demands the proclamation of the Gospel in a new way, yet the use of an older language emphasizing the dichotomy of the earthly and heavenly realms, and therefore falls short of really incarnating the Gospel in the human context . . .[15]

. . . Fails to speak to and respond to this new situation in a manner that is adequate in light of the Church's new self-understanding and mission, and the state of the modern world. Incarnating the Gospel can no longer be viewed, Richard continues, "as an unceasing reincarnation of a nucleus of divine truths and realities as if they were taken out of history and abstractly isolated into a pure state and applied to always new historical contexts."[16] Such efforts fail to be true to Vatican II's efforts to foster interaction between the Church and the world. They also fail to embrace the Council's insistence that the eschatological goal of the Church cannot be separated from here and now existence. In short, the social mission of the Church established at the Second Vatican Council, with its recognition that this mission has no natural, preordained or metaphysical end, stands in opposition to the Classical mentality. In the words of George Lindbeck, Vatican II's willingness to dialogue "with others in search for solutions to realities in themselves is an appeal beyond ready made answers" such as those proffered by the Classical world view.[17]

The shift toward a Historical Existential theological paradigm at Vatican II is primarily the result of the Council's attempt to direct theology to where people are, i.e., their lived experience, so as to be meaningful and viable to them. Also facilitating the shift in theological outlook were the renewed interest in Scripture and Christology which marked theological scholarship of the time. John W. O'Malley, S.J. describes the theological shift as follows:

> The mentality with which many of the progressive theologians and other experts approached their task was more historical than in any previous council. This mentality was the result of the revival of historical studies of the 19th century and the consequent application of historical methods to sacred subjects . . . Theologians were thus much more aware of the profound changes that had taken place in the long history of the Church than were their counterparts in earlier councils. They were also aware that many of these changes could be adequately explained in merely human terms as expressions of given culture and that they were therefore not necessarily irreversible. This keener sense of history thus permitted greater freedom in judgment that some practices or traditions might be simply anachronistic and should be modified or even eliminated . . . For the first time in an ecumenical council, therefore, doctrinal positions had to be formulated with as much concern for historical context and process as their validity in terms of traditional metaphysics.[18]

This appreciation for the historical is one of the great attributes of Vatican II's ecclesiology. It enabled the Church to address the concerns of the modern world, and facilitated efforts of discerning the "signs of the times." Again, O'Malley observes, . . . "Vatican II took greater note of the world around it than any previous council . . . The Council was fully aware, therefore, that the Church was in history and in the world, and it wanted the Church to act in accordance of that awareness."[19]

It is for this reason that the Council tended toward a Historical Existential world view. This world view recognizes that each culture has distinct sets of values and meanings. Heavily influenced by contemporary social sciences, the Historical Existential view recognizes the historical and relative character of the communication of meaning and values. It attempts to understand principles as they operate in changing contexts, not as abstract, static entities. The focus of the Historical Existential view is the particular, not the universal. Human development is seen as the product of human history, not providentialism or as the manifestation of a metaphysical type. Theology, in this world view, is conceived of as an ongoing process to be carried out in the context of contemporary human experiences. The Church is not viewed as existing for itself over and above the world, but as existing for and amid all of humanity. The challenge of ecclesiology becomes discovering ways to respond to the ever changing gift of God's self-disclosure in the world, not the promulgation and protection of inscrutable doctrines. As Bernard J. F. Lonergan, S.J., noted, the Historical Existential tendency is to see the Christian message as "not disruptive of the culture, not an alien patch superimposed upon it, but a line of development within culture."[20]

It is clear that the Council viewed the starting point for doing theology to be the Church in the world:

> The experience of past ages, the progress of the sciences, and the treasures hidden in the various forms of human culture, by all of which the nature of humanity is more clearly revealed and new roads to truth are opened, these profit the Church . . . For from the beginning of her history she has learned to express the message of Christ with the help of the ideas and terminology of various philosophers, and has tried to clarify it with their wisdom . . . her purpose has been to adapt the Gospel to the grasp of all as well as to the needs of the learned, insofar as such was appropriate. Indeed this accommodated preaching of the revealed word ought to remain the law of evangelization. For thus the ability to express Christ's message in its own way is developed in each nation, and at the same time there is fostered a living exchange between the Church and the diverse cultures of people (*Gaudium et Spes* #44).

This selfsame paragraph of *Gaudium et Spes* goes on to speak of the Church's need to seek the help of those who live in the world and are well versed in various cultural settings in her theological formulations—a further attestation that the Council no longer viewed the Church as independent of the world and beyond edification.

What ought to be clear from this assessment of Classical Essentialism and Historical Existentialism and their effects upon Vatican II is captured well by Herve' Carrier, S.J.:

Two attitudes were visible from the outset (of the Council): on the one hand, there were the supporters of a defense of the Church *ad intra* against a hostile world . . . On the other hand, there was a group that wanted to use a new perspective in analyzing the duties of the Church toward the world . . . It was . . . a question of different emphases in conception . . . based on two different types of intellectual attitude: on the one hand, the reflection on principles, which was more accustomed to deductive methods (Classicism), and on the other hand, the anthropological and pastoral approach (Historical Existential).[21]

This shift from a Classical way of thinking to a more Historical Existential way of thinking is one of the great and revolutionary steps taken by the Second Vatican Council. Such a step made it easier for the Council Fathers to articulate the faith in a manner capable of being in relationship with the contemporary world. Since the Church's teachings must correlate to the needs and experiences of every era, the shift toward Historical Existentialism can be said to sustain the task of *aggiornamento*. Again, the observation of John W. O'Malley, S.J. is illuminating:

When the documents of the Council are viewed in this light, they imply an open-endedness, a certain sense of uncompleted business. If it is true that, as times change, the Church must change with them, the process of *aggiornamento* is ongoing. By definition, it cannot be statically frozen. It implies experimentation, adaptation and keen attentiveness to the lessons of experience as we daily receive them. Those who read the documents thus must perforce clash with those whose approach is more Classicist.[22]

COMPROMISING TENSIONS AND DUALISMS

It is clear that the shift from Traditional Classical Essentialism toward Historical Existentialism accounts for much of the tension inherent in the Conciliar documents. Fr. O'Malley, once again, captures well the mood of the Council:

Distinctive of the *aggiornamento* of Vatican II in all its aspects was a keener awareness of cultural differences and the historical conditioning of all aspects of the "human side" of the face of the Church than any previous conciliar reform. This was the result of methodologies that many of the influential *peritii* brought to the formulation of the documents of the Council, whether their specialty was liturgy, the Bible, Church history, ecumenism, Church-state relations, social problems or even systematic theology. The training of most of these men had caused them to modify or move away from the so-called Classicist mentality that had traditionally marked theological disciplines. The conflict between these two mentalities underlies many of the documents of the Council and is still operative today in the debate over how to interpret them.[23]

This tension illustrates that there are parallel and parting theologies operative in the Conciliar formulations: Classical Essentialism and Historical Existentialism often co-exist side by side within the documents of Vatican II. Ultimately, however, the two theologies part, for their world views, emphases, methodologies and steps of praxis are so radically disparate. This tension will persist in the Church so long as there is no reconciliation between the two theological approaches, no alternative theological methodology, and no complete shift to one theology or the other. The failure on the part of the Council to reconcile this tension compromised the Council's net effect, for it tended to isolate or compartmentalize the two theologies rather than reconcile them. The tendency was for the bishops to revert to Classicism when discussing or appealing to the *ad intra* concerns and matters of the Church, and to utilize Historical Existentialism when describing and discussing the world, cultures and the Church's *ad extra* social mission.

The Council Fathers fell victim to the tendency of Classical Essentialism, i.e., they proffered a dualistic understanding of the Church and the world despite their efforts to overcome this very dualism. Although the Council Fathers recognized that the Church and world interpenetrate one another (*Gaudium et Spes* #40), they nonetheless concluded that their respective missions are different (*Gaudium et Spes* #42), for their proper concerns focus on two different cities, i.e., temporal versus eternal (*Lumen Gentium* #36 and *Gaudium et Spes* #43). This dualism compromises the incarnational mentality found elsewhere in the Council documents, because it continues the Classical Essentialistic notion of Church as being something somehow over and above the world with a different set of concerns and a different existence and mission unaffected by the world. Such dualism betrays the sense of transcendence proffered by scripture and the Council itself, namely transcendence as something experienced, as an event that happens to us as we are confronted by God in the here and now encounter with our neighbor. So long as the dualism persists so, too, will the Classical tendency to depict the Church's concern as existing outside the temporal-historical realm.

Such a perception tends to await for the Kingdom of God to be imposed from outside/above, compromising the Council's emphasis on working for the Kingdom in the midst of the world.[24] Betrayed is Vatican II's test of faith, i.e., our ability to be sensitive to the beyond in our midst—our ability to see Christ in others.[25] Separating religion from the world in such a manner perpetuates the perception of religion as something isolated from the needs and concerns of the world—precisely what the Second Vatican Council set out to

Epiclesis

overcome. This dualism fails to show that religion is a dimension of human experience which fosters an identity best understood not in contrast with other forms of human experience, but precisely in and through its relation with them.[26]

This work will explore how these tensions and dualisms impact the dimensions of ecclesial life indispensable to the Church's task of renewal and reform. We will explore how we as Church are to respond in fidelity to the Holy Spirit's empowering of all baptized persons into the priestly, prophetic and kingly ministry of Jesus. We will consider what implications this new emphasis on baptism has for the laity and their role in the ministry and mission of service to the People of God and in the ecclesial effort to be the sacrament of the Paschal Mystery to the world. The laity's role in the ongoing transformation of the People of God into the sacrament of the Paschal Mystery via their active role in the Eucharist will also be considered. Lastly, we will examine the role of ecclesial leaders as servants to the servants of God and the *kenosis* that will be required of them if they are to respond in fidelity to the prompting of the Holy Spirit as the Spirit directs and guides the Church toward greater unity with all persons. We conclude our introduction with the thoughts of the great ecclesiologist, Yves Congar:

> The Church can be sure that God works in it, but, because it is God and not the Church that is the principle of this holy activity, the Church has to pray earnestly for His intervention as a grace . . . the Church does not in itself have any assurance that it is doing work that will "well up to eternal life;" it has to pray for the grace of the One Who is uncreated grace, that is the absolute gift, the breath of the Father and the Word . . . This dogma means that the life and activity of the Church can be seen today as (one long and ongoing) epiclesis.[27]

NOTES

1. Yves Congar, O.P., *I Believe in the Holy Spirit Vol. I* (New York: Crossroad Publishing, 1997), 31–32.

2. Congar, *I Believe in the Holy Spirit Vol. I*, 58.

3. Congar, *I Believe in the Holy Spirit Vol. I*, 65.

4. Congar, *I Believe in the Holy Spirit Vol. I*, 170–171.

5. Gustavo Gutierrez, *A Theology of Liberation* (Maryknoll, New York: Orbis Books, 1973), 4.

6. Gutierrez, *A Theology of Liberation*, 5–6.

7. Gutierrez, *A Theology of Liberation*, 6.

8. John W. O'Malley, S.J., "Reform, Historical Consciousness And Vatican II's *Aggiornamento*," *Theological Studies* 32 (1970): 590–595.

9. R. Kevin Seasoltz, O.S.B., "The Sacred Liturgy: Development and Directions," in *Remembering The Future: Vatican II and Tomorrow's Liturgical Agenda*, ed. Carl A. Last (New York: Paulist Press, 1983), 54.

10. John W. O'Malley, S.J., *Tradition and Transition: Historical Perspectives on Vatican II* (Wilmington, Delaware: Michael Glazier, 1989), 67–68.

11. O'Malley, *Tradition and Transition*, 68–69.

12. O'Malley, *Tradition and Transition*, 69.

13. T. O'Meara, "Philosophical Models in Ecclesiology," *Theological Studies* 39 (1978): 21.

14. O'Meara, "Philosophical Models," 21.

15. Lucien Richard, O.M.I., "Mission and Inculturation: The Church in the World" in *Vatican II: The Unfinished Agenda—A Look to the Future*, eds., Lucien Richard, O.M.I., Daniel Harrington, S.J. and John W. O'Malley, S.J. (New York: Paulist Press, 1987), 106.

16. Richard, "Mission and Inculturation," 109.

17. George A. Lindbeck, *The Future of Roman Catholic Theology* (Philadelphia, Pennsylvania: Fortress Press, 1962), 48.

18. O'Malley, *Traditions and Transition*, 14.

19. O'Malley, *Traditions and Transition*, 15.

20. Bernard J. F. Lonergan, S.J., *Method in Theology* (New York: Herder and Herder, 1972), 362.

21. Herve' Carrier, S.J., "The Contribution of the Council to Culture," in *Vatican II: Assessment and Perspectives Twenty Five Years After Vol. 3*, ed. Rene' Latourelle (New York: Paulist Press, 1989), 445–446.

22. O'Malley, *Tradition and Transitions*, 30.

23. O'Malley, *Tradition and Transitions*, 30.

24. Ronald Gregor Smith, *Secular Christianity* (New York: Harper and Row Publishers, 1966), 120–122.

25. John A. T. Robinson, *Honest to God* (Philadelphia: The Westminster Press, 1963), 90.

26. Francis Schussler Fiorenza, *Foundational Theology* (New York: Crossroad, 1992), 201.

27. Yves Congar, O.P., *I Believe in the Holy Spirit Vol. III* (New York: Crossroad, 1997), 271.

Chapter One

Baptismal Dignity of the People of God

THE MINISTRY AND MISSION OF BAPTISM

The Second Vatican Council called the Church to be the sacrament of the Paschal Mystery to the world. As part of this call, "the obligation of spreading the faith is imposed upon on every disciple of Christ" (*Lumen Gentium* #17). Given that the Church strives to be a symbol of Christ in the world, it follows that members of the Church must live out their vocations specifically in the secular realm. This will be indispensable to the Church's self-realization as a sacrament. As the Church's points of contact with the world, individual members of the Church must exemplify and illuminate the Christlike life in and to the world so as to invite and to draw others to Christ. This mission and ministry of all Christians flows from baptism.

> Through baptism we are formed in the likeness of Christ . . . all of us are made members of Christ's body . . . in the building up of Christ's body various members and functions have their part to play . . . Christ continually distributes in His body . . . gifts of ministries in which, by His own power, we serve each other unto salvation (*Lumen Gentium* #'s 7–8).

In short, via baptism, Christ shares His Spirit with us so as to renew us and to enable Himself to move through us as He shares His gifts and expands His body (*Lumen Gentium* #8).

> For this reason, by no weak analogy, the Church is compared to the mystery of the Incarnate Word. As the assumed nature inseparably united to Him, serves the divine Word as a living organ of salvation, so, in a similar way, does the . . . Church serve the Spirit of Christ, who vivifies it, in the building up of the body . . . By the

power of the risen Lord the Church is given strength that it might . . . reveal to the
world . . . .the mystery of its Lord . . . *(Lumen Gentium #8)*.

BAPTISM IS A COMMUNAL PHENOMENA

Seen in such a light, it becomes clear that baptism is both an individual and
communal event. As individuals, the baptized are called to conversion to the
values and attitudes of Jesus. They are also incorporated into a community of
faith which gives witness and service to the Kingdom of God. Baptism ori-
ents persons to the wider mission and ministry of the Church.[1]

> . . . allotting His (the Spirit's) gifts to everyone according as He wills, He dis-
> tributes special graces among the faithful of every rank. By these gifts He makes
> them fit and ready to undertake the various tasks and offices which contribute
> toward the renewal and building up of the Church . . . These charisms, whether
> they be the more outstanding or the more simple and widely diffused, are to be
> received with thanksgiving and consolation for they are perfectly suited to and
> useful for the needs of the Church *(Lumen Gentium #12)*.

Vatican II's vision of Baptism is consistent with the witness of scripture
and the example of the apostolic church. Scripture presents baptism as an oc-
casion for adults and/or households who had expressed their faith in Christ to
be more fully initiated into the fledgling community of Christians committed
to the realization of the Kingdom of God announced by Jesus.[2] This initiation
rite was believed to unite one to the death and resurrection of Jesus, enabling
one to die to their old way of life and rise to a new life dedicated to the ministry and mission of Jesus, i.e., to be "ambassadors" for Christ (See Romans
6:3–11 and II Corinthians 5:16–6:2).[3] As such, the baptized became members
of and were united to a community of others who were committed to this selfsame mission and ministry (See I Corinthians 12:12–13). These Christians,
the baptized, understood themselves to be united to one another in the body
of Christ through the grace of the Holy Spirit. Although each of the baptized
were graced by the Holy Spirit, the gift that was received was understood to
be for the betterment of the entire body/community. The diversity of gifts
given to each of the baptized by the Holy Spirit were meant to serve the common good of all and to build up the Christian community (See I Corinthians
6:9–11, 12:7f and Colossians 2:12f).[4] The example of the early church is consistent in its presentation of baptism with personal conversion always con-
joined with communal commitment to the building up of the Kingdom of
God.

THE NATURE OF THE CATECHUMENATE

So central to baptism was the task of building up the community, the early church required an extensive catechetical formation process for those who would be baptized. A sponsor was assigned to the neophyte for a period of two to three years during which the catechumen's life and conduct would be scrutinized to determine if Christian *metanoia* was, indeed, unfolding in her or his life. As the culmination of the preparation process neared, during the season of Lent, the entire community would intensify and participate in final instructions and preparation of the catechumen for his/her initiation into the community over Easter weekend—an elaborate ritual which included baptism, confirmation and first Eucharist celebrated by the entire community in union with their bishop.[5] From the preparation of the candidate and the communal celebration of the ritual, we can, again, see how the early church viewed baptism as both an individual and communal phenomena.

HISTORICAL SHIFTS REGARDING
THE THEOLOGICAL EMPHASES OF BAPTISM

The interconnection between baptism and community persisted through the fourth century when several factors converged to lead baptism down a different theological path. As Christianity became the official religion of the Roman Empire in the fourth century, large numbers of people embraced Christianity at a fast and steady pace. To keep pace with the influx of converts, baptism was now entrusted to priests, whereas the bishop would confirm the baptized at a subsequent time (thus confirmation came to be disjoined from baptism). In order to ensure ongoing continuity in building up the church, infants came to be baptized—a phenomenon further advanced by Augustine's formulation of the doctrine of Original Sin and the challenges posed by the Pelagian heresy.[6] Another result of the quickly assumed norm of baptizing infants was the elimination of the prolonged catechumenate. What emerged was a new emphasis regarding the primary meaning of baptism, namely the means for remitting Original Sin. This new theological emphasis, coupled with infant baptism and the elimination of the catechumenate, took the focus of baptism off of the community and the baptized's responsibility to the community. The existentialist understanding of the sacrament as incorporation into a community which was prevalent in the early church gave way to an essentialistic interpretation of the sacrament as the emphasis on the ontological transformation of the individual recipient's wounded nature via baptism comes to usurp the communal dimensions of the sacrament. Salvation of individual souls becomes the focus of the sacrament, eclipsing communal membership, conversion and contribution to the realization of the Kingdom.

Baptism gradually came to be more and more isolated from the community, a trajectory that continued through the Scholastic period as the focus of baptism continued to be the sacrament ("work"), itself, and the one who performed it ("worker"/cleric), rather than the ethical disposition of the recipient and his/her relationship to the community. The Scholastic preoccupation was with the sacrament ("work") being performed according to the proper form, using of the proper matter, by the appropriate worker (priest). Precision of sacramental performance, as well as preoccupation with the performer of the sacrament was accentuated by the concept of sacramental character which the Scholastics associated with both baptism and holy orders. Character implies an ontological/indelible mark upon one's soul via the reception of the sacrament. Character enables/disposes one, in one's very nature, toward a particular end/goal. Baptism was understood to bestow sacramental character which ontologically changed the recipient from a child of sin to a child of Christ, disposing her or him to a life of faith. Holy orders was deemed to confer sacramental character which marked the soul of the recipient with an ontological power to act in the person of Jesus on behalf of the church. A focus which derives from such an essentialistic view tended to preoccupy itself with the privileges and prerogatives that sacramental character bestowed upon the recipients of the sacraments at the cost of the sacraments' communal significance and import. So rigid did this view become, that baptism was deemed efficacious simply if the ritual was performed appropriately by the appropriate worker, i.e., the sacrament was efficacious *ex opere operato*. Consequently, the sacrament's ritual expression and its form and matter dominated the theological concern. Such an emphasis is far from that of the early church, for the role of community is significantly compromised and the action of the recipient (*opus operans*) is jettisoned as a secondary concern.[7] This was the dominant view of baptism through the decades prior to the Second Vatican Council, when the state of the initiation sacraments was quite unclear due to the lack of good theology explaining the interconnections between the three sacraments of initiation: baptism, confirmation and Eucharist. From the fourth century on the three initiation sacraments had come to be celebrated independently of one another and the Church lacked an adequate theological explanation of their interconnection. Additionally, 20th Century influences such as Catholic Action groups which sought to push confirmation into later adolescence and/or early adulthood, concerns over indiscriminate baptism, debates within Protestantism over the sacrament, and post-war concerns over the effects of the sacrament and nationalistic ideologies further confused the issue. Roman Catholicism found itself theologically divided when it came to baptism as the Church tried to reconcile the current baptismal practice and theology understood from an essentialistic viewpoint with the early church's more existential, historical and communal emphases.[8] Given the pastoral directives of Vatican II, which sought to place the Church at the service of the world via an active lay apostolate, we can see how this controversy around baptism would only continue.

VATICAN II'S CONSIDERATION OF BAPTISM

Despite the ongoing practice of baptizing infants and the dominant Augustinian understanding of the sacrament, Vatican II proffers a pneumatic corrective to the essentialistic interpretation that had come to minimalize the sacrament's communal dimensions in that the Council tended to interpret the sacrament within an existential framework as it called for baptism to be more fully understood and celebrated as a sacrament of initiation into the ecclesial community, conferred, preferably, at the Paschal Vigil, and preceded by a catechumenate of serious content and considerable duration involving all members of the ecclesial community.

> This transition (conversion of the catechumen), which involves a progressive change of outlook and morals, should be manifested in its social implications and effected gradually during the period of catechumenate . . . In accordance with the very ancient practice of the Church, the motives for conversion should be examined . . . It is desirable that the liturgy of Lent and Paschal time should be restored in such a way that it will serve to prepare the hearts of the catechumens for the celebration of the Paschal Mystery . . . This Christian initiation . . . should not be left entirely to priests and catechists, but should be the concern of the whole Christian community . . . the catechumens must learn to cooperate actively in the building up of the Church and in its work of evangelization, both by the example of their lives and the profession of their faith (*Ad Gentes Divinitus* #'s 13–14).

This emphasis mirrors that of the New Testament and the early church for it more readily associates initiation with conversion, and accentuates the dialectic between the baptized and the community.

Perhaps the most significant teaching regarding baptism to emerge from the Council was the positing of the three-fold dignity which accompanies the sacrament:

> The faithful, by baptism, are incorporated into Christ, are placed in the People of God, and in their own way share the priestly, prophetic and kingly office of

Christ, and to the best of their ability carry on the mission of the whole Christian people in the church and in the world (*Lumen Gentium* #31).

Baptism makes every member of the church/Body of Christ a sharer in Jesus' priestly, prophetic and kingly ministries. All share in the redeeming mission of Christ.[9] Echoing the early church, Pope John Paul II interpreted the tri-fold ministry of the baptized as creating a dynamic between the individual and the community:

> The participation of the faithful in the threefold mission of Christ as priest, prophet and king finds its source in baptism, its further development in confirmation and its realization and dynamic sustenance in Holy Eucharist. It is a participation given to each member individually, inasmuch as each is one of the many who form the one Body of the Lord . . . Precisely because it derives from church communion, the sharing of the faithful in the threefold mission of Christ requires that it be lived and realized in communion and for the increase of communion itself (*Christifideles Laici* #14).

The significance and implications of this understanding of Christian dignity stemming from baptism needs to be more fully explored if the Church is to be the sacrament of the Paschal Mystery to the world, for the Church will be this sacramental reality only if each of her members does, in fact, participate in the priestly, prophetic and kingly ministry of Jesus.

BAPTISM AS INITIATION
INTO THE PRIESTLY MINISTRY OF CHRIST

Acknowledging that all baptized members of the Church share in the priestly ministry of Christ had revolutionary effects upon the liturgical and sacramental reforms called for at the Second Vatican Council. We will explore in detail the implications that the priestly ministry of the baptized has for greater lay involvement in the liturgy in the next chapter. For now, let us consider in what other manner the baptized exercise their priestly ministry at the service of the world.

The Dogmatic Constitution on the Church, *Lumen Gentium*, promulgated at Vatican II, issues a call to all members of the Church to live a life of holiness. This life of holiness is the means by which the baptized share in the priestly ministry and mission of Christ. Striving to live a life of holiness, i.e., striving to live the life of discipleship, will require and demand great sacrifice. As Dietrich Bonhoeffer noted, the life of discipleship is costly. It calls one to respond to the call of Jesus in categorical obedience, dying to one's previous life and way of living so as to be reborn and thus enabled to live the Beatitudes.[10] Here we see the *kenosis* demanded of all the baptized if they are to embrace the mission and ministry of service to others and commit themselves to being a sacrament of the Paschal Mystery. Through our daily sacrifices and "dyings," offered so that new life and a new manner of living may be born within us, others come to see the Truth of the mystery of Christ's own Passion.

The principle occasions and opportunities for lay persons to exercise discipleship come in the midst of daily life. Our life of holiness ought to unfold in the midst of our vocations and secular activities. We will explore more fully how the lay apostolate is at the service of the Church's ministry and mission in Chapter Three. For now let us note that:

> . . . all of Christ's faithful, whatever be the conditions, duties and circumstances of their lives—and indeed through all these, will daily increase in holiness if they receive all things with faith . . . In this temporal service they will manifest to all persons the love with which God loved the world . . . Therefore, all of the faithful of Christ are invited to strive for the holiness and perfection of their own proper state. Indeed they have an obligation to strive (*Lumen Gentium* #'s 41–42).

In short, the priestly dignity conferred upon all of the faithful via baptism is central to the larger ecclesiological vision and self-understanding articulated at the Second Vatican Council. To be a sacrament of Christ to the world, the Church must serve as a symbol within the world that points to and makes Christ present. Since the Church's presence in the midst of the world is perpetuated by the lay faithful, they must serve as symbols which make Christ present to the world. They can do this only if their visible actions give witness to and exemplify their Christian claims and identity. The Church can only be the sacrament of Christ to the world if all baptized persons are sacraments, evidencing and rendering Christ present in their daily life. Baptism can be seen as the sacrament which makes it possible for the Church to be a sacrament. Pope John Paul II wrote:

> The lay faithful are sharers in the priestly mission for which Jesus offered Himself on the cross . . . Incorporated in Jesus Christ, the baptized are united to Him and to His sacrifice in the offering they make of themselves and their daily activities. Speaking of the lay faithful the Council says: "For their work, prayers, and apostolic endeavors, their ordinary married and family life, their daily labor, their mental and physical relaxation, if carried out in the Spirit, and even the hardships of daily life if patiently borne—all these become spiritual sacrifices" . . . Thus as worshipers whose every deed is holy, the lay faithful consecrate the world itself to God (*Christifideles Laici* #14).[11]

Such a vision of priestly ministry corresponds to what Thomas O'Meara, O.P. refers to as the rich and diverse "primal ministries" of the New Testament period, i.e., the pluralistic contributions of all of the baptized to the nourishment and service of the ecclesial community. In his fine book, *Theology of Ministry*, Fr. O'Meara proffers a description of ministry in the early church characterized by diverse actions on behalf of the Kingdom of God performed publicly on behalf of the community and animated by the Holy Spirit.[12] Fr. O'Meara writes:

> There is no doubt that the first Christians saw the witness of their lives as a service to the Gospel (Rom. 12:1; 16:19). When we say that ministry is public, we mean that ministry normally takes on a visible and public form in words and deeds . . . We should not accept an interpretation of baptism which asserts that the main activity of the baptized is only passive . . . [13]

This vision and example of the early church lies at the heart of Vatican II's call for an expanded notion of ministry rooted in and stemming from baptism. Again, Fr. O'Meara captures well the sense of priestly dignity associated with baptism emphasized by the Council:

> Ministry begins within the Christian community, flows out of the community, and nourishes and expands the community. Many ministries are needed to sustain a community because there are many things to be done in word, sacrament, service and evangelism . . . ministry is not only the administration of churches but the enabling of the church itself to serve and to speak the grace of the Kingdom . . . Ministry is not a badge, not an office . . . but a spectrum of various concrete and helpful services to grace . . . each man and each woman is a sacrament, and serving those billions of sacraments is the liturgy of ministry (Mt. 25:41) . . . baptism also initiates a person into charism and diaconal action, into a community that is essentially ministerial.[14]

The priestly dignity of baptism is to be realized via a ministry of service directed by the Gospel and toward the renewal of the ecclesial and temporal communities. In short, all Christian ministry is to be understood as being rooted in and stemming from baptism:

> Christian ministry is the public activity of a baptized follower of Jesus Christ flowing from the Spirit's charism and an individual personality on behalf of a Christian community to proclaim, serve, and realize the Kingdom of God.[15]

BAPTISM AS INITIATION
INTO THE PROPHETIC MINISTRY OF CHRIST

Baptism also dignifies the recipient with a sharing in the prophetic ministry and mission of Jesus. The implications of this baptismal charism, too, stand in need of greater explication and more extensive praxis. Yves Congar, O.P. explained the charism thusly:

> In its widest extension the prophetical function of the Church includes all the work of the Holy Spirit in Her whereby, in Her present state of pilgrimage, She knows God and His purpose of grace, and makes them known to others.[16]

We can see that the prophetic charism encompasses all of the work of the Holy Spirit within the Church and, once revealed, demands that it be shared with others. This charism and its edification of the community was greatly valued among the ancient Jews and early Christians. The prophetic gift was assurance of God's ongoing self-disclosure to and presence within the community as they strove to discern and live according to His will. The prophet offered insights regarding the will of God which determined the lived experience of the people, affirming or challenging communal conduct and often calling for change. The loss of appreciation for this baptismal charism and ministry within the Church is unfortunate, for it is impossible to know what guidance and directives of the Holy Spirit have gone unnoticed and unimplemented as a result. Lamenting the loss of the prophetic ministry within the Church, with its message pertaining to the Kingdom of God and the transformation of society, Walter Rauschenbusch, in his seminal work, *A Theology for the Social Gospel*, wrote:

> ... theology has been deprived of the inspiration of great ideas ... The persons who have contributed the most fruitful impulses to Christian thought have been persons of prophetic vision, and their theology proved the most effective for future times ... It is impossible to estimate what inspirational impulses have been lost to theology and the Church because it did not develop the doctrine ... and see the world and its redemption from this point of view.[17]

The contemporary Church needs to discern and heed the prophetic voice within the ecclesial community, particularly when the *consensus fidelium* serves as a pneumatic corrective challenging the world to mirror the Kingdom of God and calling the Church to become more meaningful and viable to the faithful and the world. All baptized members of the Church must accept the responsibility they have as "sharers in the appreciation of the Church's supernatural faith, that cannot err in matters of belief" (*Christifideles Laici* #14). Each member is called to such discernment by the Holy Spirit so as to enable them to contribute to the renewal and building up of the Church.[18] Yves Congar spoke of the *consensus fidelium* as:

> ... infallible in the living possession of its faith ... this infallibility is not simply a submissive deference to the hierarchy, a moral act of docility and obedience, but is of vital, moral nature ...[19]

What specifically characterizes the laity is their secular nature . . . the laity, by their very vocation, seek the Kingdom of God by engaging in temporal affairs and by ordering them according to the plan of God. They live in the world, that is, in each and in all of the secular professions and occupations. They live in the ordinary circumstances of family and social life, from which the very web of their existence is woven. They are called there by God that by exercising their proper function and led by the Spirit of the Gospel they may work for the sanctification of the world from within as a leaven. In this way they make Christ known to others . . . (*Lumen Gentium* #31).

Vatican II made explicit the interconnection between the sacraments and the lay apostolate:

The apostolate of the laity is a sharing in the salvific mission of the Church. Through baptism and confirmation all are appointed to this apostolate by the Lord Himself. Moreover, by the sacraments, and especially by the Eucharist, that love of God and humanity which is the soul of the apostolate is communicated and nourished. The laity . . . are given this special vocation: to make the Church present and fruitful in those places and circumstances where it is only through them that She can become the salt of the earth. Thus, every lay person, through those gifts given to them, is at once the witness and the living instrument of the mission of the Church itself . . . (*Lumen Gentium* #33).

Strengthened by the power of the Holy Spirit in the sacrament of confirmation, it is by the Lord, Himself, that one is assigned to the lay apostolate . . . In order that one may in all one's actions bear witness to Christ the world over . . . the apostolate is . . . poured out by the Holy Spirit into the hearts of all the members of the Church . . . And the precept of charity, which is the Lord's greatest commandment, urges all Christians to work for the glory of God through the coming of His Kingdom and for the communication of eternal life to all persons, that they may know the one true God and Jesus Christ whom He has sent . . . On all Christians, accordingly, rests the noble obligation of working to bring all persons throughout the world to hear and accept the divine message of salvation (*Apostolicam Actuositatem* #3).

CONFIRMATION AS THE SEAL OF BAPTISM'S INITIATION INTO THE KINGLY MISSION OF CHRIST

The Council's association of the sacraments of initiation with the lay apostolate is consistent with the example of the early church. The interconnection between baptism and the apostolate has been compromised over time, but the theological understanding of confirmation has remained consistent throughout the Church's history. Confirmation has always been seen as the gift of the Holy Spirit to strengthen the confirmed with the grace needed to live a mature faith, give public witness, and to build up the Body of Christ.[23]

By the sacrament of confirmation the faithful are more perfectly bound to the Church and are endowed with the special strength of the Holy Spirit. Hence they are, as true witnesses of Christ, more strictly obliged to spread the faith by word and deed (*Lumen Gentium* #11).

In short, Vatican II's treatment of the sacrament of confirmation and the lay apostolate dovetail neatly. Interpreted as the sacrament of the lay apostolate, in a special way the sacrament of confirmation, given its particular charisms, can facilitate the Church's efforts to be the sacrament of the Paschal Mystery to the world.

CONCLUDING REMARKS

As the Church strives to discern the signs of the times and render herself a meaningful and life-giving sacrament of Christ to the world, a greater appreciation and utilization of the graces of baptism and the Spiritual gifts of each baptized member of the Church will have to be more fully actualized. This demands conversion on the part of both the laity and the hierarchy in terms of how the Church understands and implements power. All members of the Church must recognize that each and all of us, by virtue of baptism, share in the ministry and mission of Jesus Christ. This conversion within the Church itself will enhance her "signing" ability and thus lend to her efficaciousness as a sacrament of the Paschal Mystery. It will demand dying to old mentalities and structures and require openness to new interpretations of ministry and mission and the necessary institutional and structural mechanisms which will enable them to bear fruit and provide new life and service to the Church and world.

The laity are challenged with the awesome burden and responsibility—which is simultaneously a tremendous obligation, duty and gift—of understanding that the very self-understanding of the Church and her mission to the world, articulated by the Second Vatican Council, will succeed only to the extent that they receive, respond to and live out their baptismal dignity. Such an understanding demands that they modify the view that they have of themselves and of the clergy. The ministry and mission of the Church must come to be seen as a shared responsibility, not solely the responsibility of the clergy. The laity will have to put this new understanding into praxis by assuming more active and meaningful roles within the Church, and by consciously choosing to live their lives in such a way as to render the Church's share in the salvific and redeeming ministry and mission of Christ explicit to the world.

The clergy, too, will be challenged by the needed conversion of mentalities and action. They, too, will have to recognize and embrace the ministerial and missionary tasks of the Church as a shared responsibility with the laity. They will have to allow for and make possible greater realization of the graces of baptism by affording the baptized greater and more authoritative roles in Church practices and ecclesial structures, and allow for and facilitate greater lay initiatives in carrying out the Church's salvific and redeeming ministry and mission via their apostolate of social justice.

This conversion would yield a dialectic of mutual and reciprocated trust, support, edification, challenge and praxis between the laity and clergy. If both the laity and the clergy respond to this challenge and call for conversion, their actions will reveal the Paschal Mystery. Out of our suffering and struggle experienced in redefining ourselves and the Church in this manner we will reveal to the world the truth that new life, indeed, can be born out of death. In reciprocating trust and respect for one another by acknowledging our shared ministry and mission as baptized members of the Church, clergy and laity will evidence the *kenotic* love of Christ as they surrender to and empty themselves of their old understandings and practices and embrace a new scenario which embraces a shared baptismal dignity, a shared authority within the institutional structures and mechanism of the Church, and a shared responsibility to perpetuate the ministry and mission of Christ in the world. Such a conversion on the part of the laity and clergy will show forth to all the truth of the Resurrection—that out of suffering and death a new and transformed mode of existence animated and sustained by the Holy Spirit can emerge and bring new hope, new life to the Church and to the world.

NOTES

1. Gregory L. Klein, O.Carm. and Robert A. Wolfe, O.Carm., *Pastoral Foundations of the Sacraments* (New York: Paulist Press, 1998), 56 and 59.

2. Liam Kelly, *Sacraments Revisited* (New York: Paulist Press, 1998), 34.

3. Kelly, *Sacraments Revisited*, 35–36.

4. Yves Congar, O.P., *I Believe in the Holy Spirit Vol. I* (New York: Crossroad 1997), 34–35.

5. Anscar J. Chupungco, *Sacraments and Sacramentals* (Collegeville, MN: The Liturgical Press, 2000), 5–25.

6. Any number of quality survey texts are available proffering historical overviews of the development of the sacraments.

7. Ibid.

8. Ibid.

9. See Vatican II's *Lumen Gentium* #33 and Pope John Paul II, *Christifideles Laici* #'s 13 and 23.

10. See Dietrich Bonhoeffer, *The Cost of Discipleship* (New York: Touchstone, 1995).

11. Thomas F. O'Meara, O.P., *Theology of Ministry* (New York: Paulist Press, 1999), 45–49.

12. O'Meara, *Theology of Ministry*, 139–149.

13. O'Meara, *Theology of Ministry*, 142–144.

14. O'Meara, *Theology of Ministry*, 146–147.

15. O'Meara, *Theology of Ministry*, 150.

16. Yves Congar, O.P., *Lay People in the Church* (Westminster, Maryland: Christian Classics, Inc., 1985), 271.

17. Walter Rauschenbusch, *A Theology for the Social Gospel* (Nashville: Abingdon Press, 1987), 137.

18. See Vatican II's *Lumen Gentium* #12.

19. Congar, *Lay People in the Church*, 289.

20. Congar, *Lay People in the Church*, 298.

21. Such teachings can be found in the corpus of social encyclicals written over the course of the past century which comprise Catholic Social Thought.

22. Congar, *Lay People in the Church*, 262–263.

23. Any number of quality survey texts provide historical overviews of the development of the sacrament of confirmation.

Chapter Two

The Eucharist, The Laity and The Church's Apostolate of Justice

THE EUCHARIST AND THE CHURCH'S SOCIAL MISSION ARE INTIMATELY CONNECTED

As the Church strives to be the sacrament of the Paschal Mystery of Christ and the servant to all of humanity, all of the faithful will need the graces of the sacraments to sustain them in their efforts. Chief among the sacraments is the Eucharist. Within the Eucharist we recall the Paschal Mystery of Christ, pledge ourselves to Christ, and receive the grace of His Paschal Mystery which empowers us to be servants unto others. In the Eucharist we encounter the One of whom we are called to be a sacrament. Through the grace of the sacrament Jesus makes Himself actively present among us in a tangible way by extending among us on earth in visible form the saving grace of His Paschal Mystery.

Edward Schillebeeckx, O.P., in his seminal work, *Jesus The Sacrament Of The Encounter With God*, describes the sacraments as earthly extensions of the Body of Christ which enable us to encounter Christ and bring us into contact with the saving power of Christ, leaving us transformed by the encounter.[1] Once transformed by the encounter with Christ in the sacrament, we are all impelled to share the experience with others. Similarly, describing the assembled Church gathered for the Eucharist, Gordon Lathrop states that:

> In these things the Church is filled with the power of the Spirit to bear witness in the world to the truth about God. The meeting for worship is itself the ground and beginning of such witness. The meeting for worship is the church becoming church.[2]

The Second Vatican Council and Pope John Paul II echo these sentiments in declaring: "The Eucharist is the summit toward which the activity of the

Church is directed; it is also the fount from which all her power flows"
(*Sacrosanctum Concilium* #10). The sacraments, particularly the Eucharist,
are what make the church, bestow grace upon the faithful, and challenge and
empower us for the apostolate.

> From this source (the liturgy) the Church, equipped with the gifts of its Founder
> and faithfully guarding His precepts of charity, humility and self-sacrifice, re-
> ceives the mission to proclaim and to spread among all peoples the Kingdom of
> Christ and of God and to be, on earth, the initial budding forth of that Kingdom
> (*Lumen Gentium* #5).

> It is the liturgy through which, especially in the divine sacrifice of the Eucharist,
> the work of our redemption is accomplished, and it is through the liturgy, espe-
> cially, that the faithful are enabled to express in their lives and manifest to oth-
> ers the mystery of Christ and the real nature of the true Church (*Sacrosanctum
> Concilium* #2).

> . . . I wish to briefly reaffirm the fact that the Eucharist constitutes the soul of
> all Christian life. In fact, Christian life is expressed in the fulfilling of the great-
> est commandment, that is to say, in the love of God and neighbor, and this love
> finds its source in the Blessed Sacrament . . . the Eucharist signifies this charity,
> and therefore recalls it, makes it present and at the same time brings it about
> . . . there also springs up within us a lively response of love . . . we enter upon
> the path of love . . . and serve the love to which we are called to in Jesus Christ
> (*Dominicae Cenae* #5).

> Receiving the Bread of Life, disciples of Christ ready themselves to undertake with
> the strength of the Risen Lord and His Spirit the tasks which await them in their or-
> dinary life. For the faithful who have understood the meaning of what they have
> done, the Eucharistic celebration does not stop at the church door. Like the first wit-
> nesses of the Resurrection, Christians who gather each Sunday to experience and
> proclaim the presence of the Risen Lord are called to evangelize and bear witness
> in their daily lives . . . Once the assembly disperses, Christ's disciples return to their
> everyday surroundings with the commitment to make their whole life a gift . . . not
> unlike the disciples of Emmaus who, once they had recognized the Risen Lord in
> the breaking of the bread, felt the need to return immediately to share with their
> brothers and sisters the joy of meeting the Lord (*Dominicae Cenae* #45).

The interconnection which exists between the Eucharist and the Church's
mission of service to the world is recognized by all Christians. The ecumenical statement of the World Council of Churches states:

> The Eucharist embraces all aspects of life . . . The Eucharistic celebration de-
> mands reconciliation and sharing among all those regarded as brothers and sis-
> ters in the one family of God and is a constant challenge in search for appropri-
> ate relationships in social, economic and political life. All kinds of injustice,

racism, separation and lack of freedom are radically challenged when we share in the body and blood of Christ . . . As participants in the Eucharist, therefore, we prove inconsistent if we are not actively participating in the ongoing restoration of the world's situation and the human condition . . . Solidarity in the Eucharistic communion of the body of Christ and responsible care of Christians for one another and the world find specific expression in the liturgies . . . Christians are called in the Eucharist to be in solidarity with the outcast and to become signs of the love of Christ . . . The very celebration of the Eucharist is an instance of the Church's participation in God's mission to the world. This participation takes everyday form in the . . . service of neighbor, and faithful presence in the world (Lima Document #'s 20–25).

In short, it is the sacraments, especially the Eucharist (the "principal manifestation of the Church" [*Sacrosanctum Concilium* #41]), which enables the Church, herself, to be a sacrament, by affording the faithful the grace needed to live in the midst of the world in a way that reveals Christ. Roger Haight, S.J., elucidates:

Sacraments above all are meant to nurture and sustain faith . . . Faith is a commitment of one's life which plays itself out in praxis, so that informed action or praxis is the deepest carrier of faith itself. Hence the sacraments which sustain faith have their primary efficacy in the way a person leads his or her life. This efficacy is thus historical; it consists in the praxis of each person's life and in the common public behavior of the whole community . . . the effectivity of the sacraments is to be measured by their historical efficacy, the change that is wrought through them in the lives of the recipients . . .[3]

Given the interconnection between the Eucharist and the practice of social justice, Christopher Kiesling, O.P., noted:

The effectiveness of this sacrament to achieve what it signifies is conditioned by us, members of the Church; if we are not working for underlying justice, the Church's sacramentality is frustrated in regard to efficacy and eventually obscured even as a sign.[4]

In short, "the true test of the authenticity of sacramental practice is the Christian life which it engenders."[5]

The Pneumatic corrective proffered by the Liturgical Movement and the Second Vatican Council called for the Church to recover these truths about liturgical worship. Such an understanding of the sacramental life is born out of a historical existential vision which views the sacraments and social praxis as intricately related. The Eucharist is the gathered assembly drawn together to proclaim and celebrate the mysteries of the faith. It also culminates in a sending forth of the faithful to embark upon the mission of manifesting God's

will in their daily lives, i.e., to "go forth in peace to love and serve the Lord."[6]
Again, Reverend Lathrop captures well the two-fold nature of Eucharist as assembly and mission:

> The practice of Christian holiness, then, has a two-fold character. It involves the
> continuous reconstitution of assembly in communion with all the other assemblies
> of Christians . . . and a constant extension into daily life of practices
> learned in the practice of gathering. It involves seriousness about the meeting
> and what flows from the meeting . . . In Christ, holiness is connection with others
> . . . and transformative of the world.[7]

In short, "the meeting is to become a paradigm of God's intention for the
world, a sign of God's own holiness."[8]

The tendency within the Christian tradition, as we will see, was for the
sacrament's dual focus to be compromised due to the theological tensions discussed
in the Introduction. As the Church moved beyond the apostolic period
and its historical existential sacramental emphases, an essentialistic sacramentology
evolved which tended to divide the foci of the Eucharist, i.e., it
tended to separate the *ad intra* dimensions of the sacrament from its *ad extra*
dimensions. As a result, the interconnection between the Eucharistic assembly
and the apostolate of mission and ministry to the world was compromised.

LITURGY AS SCHOOL OF SOCIAL VIRTUES

The Eucharist can be said to be both world-making[9] and a catechetical event
that teaches justice.[10] Liturgical symbols function to challenge participants to
see the ultimate value and meaning of society. The liturgy provides the faithful
with a story, vision, and imaginative view of the world based upon the life,
death and resurrection of Christ. R. Kevin Seasoltz, O.S.B., explains:

> The liturgy lays out a series of verbal and non-verbal symbols and puts us
> through a series of actions which shape our attitudes toward God, toward ourselves,
> toward one another and toward life in general . . . Liturgy is about creating
> persons and communities in the image and likeness of God . . . Liturgical
> rites are meant to convey attitudes and dispositions . . . They are meant to put us
> in proper relationships with ourselves, others in the community, and God.[11]

According to Paul J. Wadell, C.P., the word of God which we encounter in
the liturgy presents us with the language of God. The liturgy serves as the vehicle
by which we learn God's language. To be a Christian is to accept the
word of God and embrace the life of discipleship to which it calls us.[12]

The Christian moral life is the steadfast commitment to learn the language of God that comes to us in Christ, to embody it, and to witness it to the world . . . As we speak this language of God we are formed in it, and as we live it out we become one with it.[13]

Gordon Lathrop echoes these sentiments regarding the liturgical assembly as venue for the language of God when he calls for Christian eschatology to serve the purposes of the Gospel by serving the needs of current humanity:

Christian faith . . . ought provide a rich field of images that . . . express the seriousness of history, the acuteness of human need, the limits within which we all live, the merciful action of God to transform us within those limits, and the church as an assembly of witness to that action . . . From the point of view of practice, the intention of the images is to enable our participation in the assembly-event. They give us a way to imagine what we are doing and so to follow our imagination . . . [14]

Additionally, Lathrop explains:

Christian worship has cultural characteristics. It has its own identity-giving and world-interpreting structures, and yet the meanings and identity it conveys belong to Christians who live within many actual cultures. Thus Christianity is most frequently a symbol-system in contrast to or in cooperation with surrounding symbol-systems, perhaps exercising influence upon those systems, perhaps utterly unrelated to them . . . Christians believe that God can transform our varying means of communication into bearers of saving grace, can inhabit and dwell amidst our symbol-systems. This is always happening . . . [15]

This language of God, and the life to which it calls us, is evidenced in the liturgy in a plethora of ways: preaching, prayers, readings, songs, exchange of peace, etc. The agreed upon statement of the World Council of Churches, *One Baptism, One Eucharist, and a Mutually Recognized Ministry*, captures well this potential of the Eucharist:

Solidarity in the Eucharistic communion of the body of Christ and responsible concern of Christians for one another and the world should be given specific expression in the liturgy, for example, in the mutual forgiveness of sins; the kiss of peace; the bringing of the gifts . . . a specific prayer for the needy and suffering . . . the taking of the Eucharist to the sick and to those in prison. All these manifestations of love in the Eucharist are directly related to Christ's own testimony as a servant, in whose servant-hood Christians themselves participate by virtue of their union with Him. As God in Christ has entered into the human situation, so Eucharistic liturgy should be near the concrete and particular situations of humanity . . . Mission is more than a consequence of the Eucharist. Whenever the Church is the Church, mission must be part of its life.[16]

In short, the liturgy teaches us the missionary task of our apostolate. Again, the words of Kevin Seasoltz are illuminating:

> The liturgy provides a context in which the celebrants can discover or rediscover who they are in the world and what the nature of their world actually is. If the liturgy is celebrated as it should be celebrated, the celebrants are invited to experience themselves as persons relating to God, to others in the community and to the world as a whole. Social consciousness inevitably impinges on their lives.[17]

Thus, the Eucharist can be said to be the stage where Christian identity is acted out.[18] James L. Empereur, S.J., and Christopher G. Kiesling, O.P., expound:

> The liturgy is the climatic expression of the spiritual life of the Church. It is the way that the Christian community symbolically re-enacts its relationship with God. This liturgical spirituality implies the actual participation in the mission of the Church as a means of opening ourselves to the saving power of Christ and the transforming actions of the Spirit. This spirituality is a concrete way of living the Gospel under the inspiration of the same Spirit. There is, then, a direct relationship between social justice and the way liturgical spirituality leads the Christian to experiences of transcendence.[19]

As an experience of grace, the liturgy ought to direct participants toward appropriate Christian praxis. The symbols of the liturgy demand that we appropriate their challenging meaning into our lives. Therefore, the sacraments must come to deal with the complexity of the lives of Christians in the twenty first century so that their meaning will perpetually motivate us to service of others. Worship ought to give us cause to reflect on our relations with others, and our praxis ought to reveal that we accept what is offered in our worship.[20] Symbols work when they entice people to enter into them, perceive themselves as part of them, and project a course of conduct.[21] If we truly understood that the Eucharist was Christ's presence among us we should understand that the only adequate response to our worship is participation in Christ's work for others.[22] In sum, a historical existential approach to the sacraments recognizes that:

> The more completely the expression of cultures are taken over for the liturgy, the more closely the language and symbols of the liturgy correspond with the social features of a period, the more likely it is that celebrations of the liturgy will have secondary effects which will be felt in the life of society outside of worship. When this happens the liturgy can perform its function of providing meaning and motivations which will help shape the lives, not only of individual be-

lievers, but also of the whole believing community and go on to influence the wider society outside.[23]

NECESSITY OF LAY PARTICIPATION IN THE EUCHARIST

If the liturgy is to be a source of inspiration for our missionary task in the world, as well as the venue in which we encounter the Lord and receive His grace, then our participation in the liturgy is of utmost importance. Vatican II's reform of the liturgy was dedicated precisely to this aim. The Council Fathers called for the full, conscious and active participation of all of the faithful in the celebration of the Eucharist (See *Sacrosanctum Concilium* #'s 14, 30 and 48). Since the Eucharist renders present the victory and triumph of Christ (See *Sacrosanctum Concilium* #6), instructs, nourishes and elevates the faithful (See *Sacrosanctum Concilium* #33 and *Ad Gentes Divinitus* #15), motivates pastoral activity, and makes Christ present, the Second Vatican Council called for the liturgy to be simple, short, clear and within the faithful's powers of comprehension (See *Sacrosanctum Concilium* #34).

> In the restoration and promotion of the sacred liturgy the full and active participation by all of the people is the aim to be considered before all else, for it is the primary and indispensable source from which the faithful are to derive the Christian Spirit (*Sacrosanctum Concilium* #14).

In order to have all of the faithful more actively involved in the Eucharist, the Council not only called for liturgical inculturation (See *Sacrosanctum Concilium* #'s 37–40) and the use of the vernacular (See *Sacrosanctum Concilium* #'s 36 and 54), but also softened the lay-cleric distinction which for centuries had tended to view the cleric as the active liturgical agent and the laity as its passive observers. We have already seen how the Council did much to recover the communal nature of the liturgy. Additionally, we have explored the significance of the Council's understanding of baptism as an initiation into the priestly, prophetic and kingly ministries of Jesus. From the priestly dignity of baptism stems a greater appreciation of the role that the laity have in the celebration of the Eucharist: "The faithful, in virtue of their royal priesthood, join in the offering of the Eucharist" (*Lumen Gentium* #10).

> Taking part in the Eucharistic sacrifice, which is the fount and apex of the whole Christian life, the faithful offer the divine Victim to God, and offer themselves along with it. Thus . . . all take part in the liturgical service (*Lumen Gentium* #11).

In pursuing its own salvific purpose not only does the Church communicate divine life to humanity but in a certain sense it casts the reflected light of that divine life over all of the earth, notably in the way it heals and elevates the dignity of the human person, in the way it consolidates human society, and endows the daily activity of persons with a deeper sense and meaning (*Gaudium et Spes* #40).

The Council recognized that the full realization of humanity could only come about in and through culture from which the church can draw values and other benefits to her own task and mission.

If the Church is to be successful in rendering the Eucharist intelligible to the faithful, and if she is to be successful in connecting the sacramental life with the apostolate, then she must be open to pluralism and diversity, for the experiences of the faithful, their cultures and their needs vary from place to place. Again, Reverend Lathrop explains:

> . . . diversity in the practice of the churches is not necessarily wrong, nor is it necessarily destructive of unity. Such diversity can be a sign of fidelity and a mysterious gift of mutual enrichment, as the gospel of Jesus Christ is celebrated in different places in different ways.[28]

The Church ought not presume to have a single uniform means of liturgical worship, nor should she presume that the needs and tasks of the apostolate of service to the world are the same in each and all contexts. Instead, she must allow herself flexibility in both her sacramental celebrations and disciplines, and her actions in pursuit of social justice. Once more, Reverend Lathrop explains:

> The assemblies in many different places are one because they are engaged in the life of the one triune God by the use of one Baptism, the hearing of the one Word, the celebration of one table . . . The assemblies are the catholic church because they do these things in ever new cultural situations, according to the dignity of each local place, bringing the gifts of lands and peoples into the unity that links all assemblies across time and space.[29]

Again, we see the need for the Church to embrace a *kenosis*, i.e., she needs to empty herself of the ecclesiological vision of the Classical Essentialistic world view which viewed the Church as over and above the world, immune from the conditions of the world, and universally uniform in identity and praxis. The Church must have the courage to embrace the Historical Existential view which sees the catholicity/universality of the Church, as well as her meaningfulness and viability, as necessitating multiple expressions, manifestations and praxis, in order to meet the needs of the faithful in diverse situations. Unity is to be realized in the midst of diversity! *Gaudium et Spes* elaborates:

> . . . the Church is not unaware how much it has profited from the history and development of humankind. It profits from the experience of past ages, from the progress of the sciences, and from the riches hidden in various cultures, through which greater light is thrown on the nature of the human person and new avenues to truth are opened up. The Church learned early in its history to express the Christian message in the concepts and language of different peoples and tried to clarify it in the light of the wisdom of their philosophers: it was an attempt to adapt the Gospel to the understanding of all persons . . . Indeed, this kind of adaptation and preaching of the revealed Word must ever be the law of all evangelization. In this way it is possible to create in every country the possibility of expressing the message of Christ in suitable terms and to foster vital contact and exchange between the Church and different cultures (*Gaudium et Spes* #44).

> . . . the Church has existed through the centuries in varying circumstances and has utilized the resources of different cultures in its preaching to spread and to explain the message of Christ, to examine and understand it more deeply, and to express it more perfectly in the liturgy and in various aspects of the life of the faithful (*Gaudium et Spes* #58).

Such adaptation and renewal was at the heart of Vatican II's task of *aggiornamento* and commitment to "reading the signs of the times."

RETURNING TO THE SCRIPTURAL AND APOSTOLIC EXAMPLE: OVERCOMING AN ESSENTIALISTIC SACRAMENTOLOGY

Scripture evidences a vision of the Church and sacraments which associates worship with the ministry and mission of service, involves all members of the community in liturgical celebrations, and is at peace with the varying customs and practices of various ecclesial communities.

Throughout the writings of the Hebrew Scriptures one is provided with a consistent framework in which to assess liturgical activity. This framework insists that worship of God cannot and ought not be severed from compassionate service to others — "Like the Word of God in history, the liturgy is the revelation of God's justice in both event and word."[30] The Hebrew Scriptures present Yahweh as a God Who is full of compassion for the poor and Who serves as their vindicator. After the Exodus, by which God delivered the Hebrews from their oppression in Egypt, the Hebrews were entrusted with the

Law as their means to properly imitate and respond to the justice of God. The code by which God's covenant was to be honored by the Hebrews is dominated by social laws and prescriptions at the service and protection of the poor and oppressed. Failure on the part of the Hebrews to adhere to the Law warranted God's condemnation and punishment. The penalties for grievances against the covenant were so severe because God was utilizing the Hebrew people as the means by which divine justice was to be revealed to all peoples. This selfsame task is the one envisioned for the Church at Vatican II in the Council's concept of the Church serving as sacrament of Christ to the world.[31] The Church, like the ancient Israelites, is to reveal, communicate, spread and manifest the justice of Christ to all cultures of the modern world.[32]

Perhaps there is no more explicit articulation of this demand to keep one's liturgical and social lives interconnected than that found in the prophetic writings of the Hebrew Scriptures. The prophets consistently associate the Hebrew's responsibility of evidencing Yahweh's justice to others with their directives pertaining to cultic activities. Describing a social situation not unlike our own, the prophets denounce their peers for both their social conduct, as well as for their misguided audacity in approaching God via cultic activities while perpetuating and tolerating social evils. Because of the wider context of social injustice, rather than being a source of edification for the people, the cultic activities repulse God and reap His condemnation upon the people:

> Woe to those who yearn for the day of the Lord . . . I hate, I spurn your feasts, I take no pleasure in your solemnities; Your cereal offerings I will not accept, nor consider your stall-fed peace offerings. Away with your noisy songs! I will not listen to the melodies of your harps. But if you would offer me holocausts, then let justice surge like water and goodness like an unfailing stream (Amos 5:18, 21–24).

> For it is love that I desire, not sacrifice, and knowledge of God rather than holocausts (Hosea 6:6).

The New Testament suggests that the early Christian's understanding of the Eucharist was, likewise, intimately united with communal responsibilities. The example of Christ was their point of departure in formulating their Eucharistic practices. Jesus' occasions of meal fellowship utilized the Jewish notion of meal as a source of solidarity and the rich Jewish traditions of meal as time of thanksgiving, blessing and remembrance of the saving acts of God in human history.[33] As with traditional Jewish meals, meal fellowship was understood by the early Christians to render present that which was promised by Christ. Saint Paul conveys this in his first letter to the Corinthians. Paul argues that since Jesus was not only the founder of the community of believers, but also in a real sense the community itself, the community of believers is, therefore, entrusted with the responsibility of making the saving reality of Christ present to the world.[34] According to Paul, celebrating the Eucharist is a participation in the Body of Christ. Remembering Jesus via the celebration incorporates an acceptance of the responsibility of extending the saving mission of Jesus.[35]

> Therefore, whoever eats the bread or drinks the cup of the Lord unworthily will have to answer for the body and blood of the Lord. A person should examine himself, and so eat the bread and drink the cup. For anyone who eats and drinks without discerning the body, eats and drinks judgment upon oneself (I Corinthians 11:27–39).

Jerome Murphy-O'Connor sheds light on the Pauline notion of Eucharistic *anamnesis* when he writes: "In the active remembrance of total commitment to Christ the past is made real in the present and its power is released to shape the future."[36]

The gospels, too, evidence how the early Christians viewed the Eucharistic meal and assembly as an event of fellowship, nourishment, transformation and mission. In Mark's gospel the Eucharistic meal serves as an invitation from Jesus to share in His suffering—the condition of the new covenant being offered by Jesus being a willingness to share in His destiny, i.e., a willingness to imitate Him.[37] Throughout the gospel of Luke meals are utilized as occasions of fellowship. Those who share the Eucharistic meal must be willing to make the commitment that such participation implies, i.e., not only performing the ritual or recalling the historical memory of the Jesus Event, but making the same self-gift that Jesus made.[38] John's gospel replaces the institution of the Eucharistic *anamnesis* with the episode of Jesus washing the feet of the disciples. Here, the Eucharist-mission-of-service link is explicitly acted out by Christ.

> So when He had washed their feet and put His garments back on and reclined at table again, He said to them, "Do you realize what I have done for you? . . . I have given you a model to follow, so that as I have done for you, you should also do" (John 13:12–15).

The example of Christ as servant is followed by a Last Supper discourse in which Jesus promises the disciples the gift of the Spirit which will be given to them so as to empower them to love others as He loved them. Other Eucharistic allusions in John's gospel also bring to mind saving actions in history—the Bread of Life Discourse and references of Jesus as the lamb of God bring to mind the saving deeds wrought by God in Hebrew history at the time of the Exodus and subsequent period of desert wandering. The Eucharist is meant to be an ongoing extension of God's saving activity in human history. Confirmation of such conviction among the Jews and early Christians is attested to by the uninterrupted repetition of the practices.[39]

Such a vision of the Eucharist continued through early patristic times.[40] Justin Martyr taught that to partake of the Eucharist was an acceptance to live as Christ had commanded, i.e., caring for the poor and serving those in need.[41] John Chrysostom reminded the community of faithful that since Jesus invited all to His table—even sinners—we, too, must receive all into our community. How can we sincerely celebrate the Eucharist knowing that Jesus gave Himself up for us, yet we don't even give up some of our food and belongings to others? Can we claim to be truly remembering and celebrating Christ if we despise and neglect the poor among us? To do so, Chrysostom maintains, is to come to the Eucharist unworthily and to receive nothing from it.[42] St. Basil argued similarly in his call for the faithful who receive the Eucharist to share the disposition of the one Who they receive.[43] Augustine maintained that the "faithful know the body of Christ (the Eucharist) if they do not neglect the body of Christ (the community)" and that via the Eucharist the faithful are enabled to continue the life of Christ for they are enlivened by His presence in the Eucharist.[44] Such sentiments were echoed by Cyril of Alexandria and others.

However, from the Early Middle Ages, through the Protestant Reformation, and up to the Second Vatican Council, the communal and missionary dimensions of worship gave way to what can be called the privatization of worship within the Roman Tradition. This evolution was largely the result of an ever increasing shift to an essentialistic world view. Ralph A. Keifer notes that this heritage of privatized worship:

> . . . concentrated far more on sacramental activity as special avenue of access to the sacred than as disclosing the event of God in the world . . . A special sphere of activity that gives special access to the realm of the sacred.[45]

Furthermore, with the legalization of Christianity in the fourth century the Eucharist came to be seen as a liturgy, i.e., a public work or service done on behalf of and for the people. The privatization of worship as a work performed for the people was further advanced by an ecclesial view which "was all the more dramatized by a progressive heightening of the sense of difference between the primary agents of the cult (clergy) and the ordinary worshiper (laity).[46] With the gradual evolution of a more highly organized ecclesial structure headed by *episcopos* and *presbteroi*, coupled with secular authority being entrusted to bishops in civil matters (with the corresponding garb and dignitary signs), the distinction between clergy and laity only polarized further. Such structural evolution compromised the laity's involvement in the Eucharist, the sense of Eucharist as communal meal, and the apostolate which was to extend out from the Eucharistic assembly. In their place came ritualization and standardization (fourth thru seventh centuries) of the Eucharist which became increasingly rigid and uniform. The introduction of Latin (fourth century) at the expense of the vernacular additionally compromised the laity's participation in the Eucharist. Even the state built basilicas architecturally bespoke of the lay-cleric distinction. Modeled on state judicial buildings, the layout emphasized watching over participating. Soon sacramentaries emerged which clarified presidential roles, prayers, rubrics, etc.— with the Roman model of liturgy coming to be deemed the standard by which all other liturgical celebrations were to be measured.

Theological developments also served to redefine Eucharistic custom. In response to the Arian controversy of the fourth century the Council of Nicea declared that Jesus was *homousious* with God the Father. As a result, an appreciation for the divinity of Christ escalated among the faithful. This heightened awareness of Christ's divinity meshed with the belief in Eucharistic real presence to create a sense of unworthiness among the faithful and a radical decline in Eucharistic reception, and the rise of multiple devotions to the Eucharistic species. Eucharist as fellowship meal came to be eclipsed by preoccupation with the moment when Jesus became present in the Eucharistic species. In short, devotionalism came to replace participation.

What evolved was a vision of the Eucharist as an event overseen and conducted by a privileged class within the church according to a precise ritual which rendered the divinity of Christ present. These sentiments combined with the location of the altar at the rear of the church with the cleric confecting the Eucharist with his back to the assembly, the erection of altar rails, and the denial of the Eucharistic cup to the laity and insistence upon reception of the host in the mouth rather than by hand (for the few who in fact communed), created a scenario in which the laity passively observed the Eucharistic activity of the clergy. So compromised was the community's involvement in the Eucharist that private masses proliferated in the eleventh century. Participation in the Eucharist reached such a low point that the Fourth Lateran Council, in 1215, had to decree that it was necessary for the faithful to receive the Eucharist at least once a year.[47] The Eucharist had become the domain of the clergy!

This monopolization of the Eucharist by the clergy would continue and reach its climax in the systematic expression of clerical powers articulated in the thirteenth century. Scholasticism tended to champion the lay-cleric distinction with its notions of sacramental character and transubstantiation. The

consider more fully in Chapters 4–6 the *kenosis* that is needed if the hierarchical and ordained leadership of the Roman Catholic Church is to be faithful to such a vision of ministry as servant-leadership.

The polarization between the laity and the clergy which has resulted from an essentialistic vision of ministry could be bridged if the directives of Vatican II for greater lay participation in the sacramental life were implemented and the shared dignity of baptism was more greatly realized. Additionally, the chasm between clergy and laity could be lessened if the laity had more proactive roles, not only in sacramental participation, but in the selection of clergy. The shared statement of the World Council of Churches, *One Baptism, One Eucharist, and a Mutually Recognized Ministry*, illuminates this possibility:

> In order to experience and demonstrate the truth that setting apart is not to some superior level of discipleship, but rather to service within the Church, it is important that the entire process of ordination involve the whole body of the people. There needs to be continual emphasis on the fact that ordination is not only "over against" nor vis-a-vis the congregation, but rather, that a person is addressed in the midst of the people. It is also important that the congregation have a part in the calling, choosing and training of the ordinand, preserving the basic significance of the call to ministry. This means more than the inclusion of a sentence or two in the liturgy and ordaining in the presence of the laity . . . (#48).

Such practices are in harmony with the apostolic example of worship as a shared communal event, and with the early church's refusal to embrace general ordinations.[50]

CONCLUSION

If the Eucharist is to transform the Church into the sacrament of the Paschal Mystery and the faithful into servants of all humanity, then the Eucharistic celebration and the plethora of ministries active within the celebration will have to be transformed to better actualize shared ministry between clergy and laity, more acutely accentuate the social implications of the celebration, and embrace cultural aspects and dimensions which render the liturgy more intelligible and meaningful.

> As a sacramental community, the church should signify in its own internal structure the salvation whose fulfillment it announces. Its organization ought to serve this task . . . If we conceive of the Church as a sacrament of salvation to the world, then it has all the more obligation to manifest in its visible structures the message that it bears.[51]

Such internal modification will challenge all of the faithful, clergy and laity alike, to be open to *kenosis* and conversion as the Holy Spirit leads the church in this process of transformation leading unto service to the world.

NOTES

1. Edward Schillebeeckx, O.P., *Christ the Sacrament of the Encounter with God* (New York: Sheed and Ward, 1963), 14–15; 54; 80.

2. Gordon Lathrop, *Holy People: A Liturgical Ecclesiology* (Minneapolis, Minnesota: Fortress Press, 1999), 9.

3. Roger Haight, S.J., *An Alternative Vision: An Interpretation of Liberation Theology* (New York: Paulist Press, 1985), 189.

4. Christopher Kiesling, O.P., "Social Justice in the Eucharistic Liturgy," *Living Light* Vol. 17, No. 1 (Spring 1980): 17.

5. Haight, *An Alternative Vision*, 205.

6. See *Sacrosanctum Concilium* #'s 3 and 6 and *Ad Gentes Divinitus* #'s 9, 15 and 36.

7. Lathrop, *Holy People*, 210–211.

8. Lathrop, *Holy People*, 212–213.

9. Dianne Bergant, C.S.A., "Liturgy and Scripture: Creating a New World," in *Liturgy and Social Justice: Celebrating Rites—Proclaiming Rights*, ed. Edward M. Grosz (Collegeville, Minnesota: The Liturgical Press, 1989), 12.

10. Gilbert Ostdiek, O.F.M., "Liturgical Catechesis and Justice" in *Living No Longer for Ourselves: Liturgy and Justice in the Nineties*, ed. Kathleen Hughes, R.S.C.J. and Mark R. Francis, C.S.V. (Collegeville, Minnesota: The Liturgical Press, 1991), 178–179.

11. R. Kevin Seasoltz, O.S.B., "Liturgy and Social Consciousness" in *To Do Justice and Right Upon the Earth*, ed. Mary E. Stamps (Collegeville, Minnesota: The Liturgical Press, 1993), 53–54.

12. Paul J. Wadell, C.P., "What Do All Those Masses Do For Us?: Reflections on the Christian Moral Life and the Eucharist" in *Living No Longer For Ourselves: Liturgy and Justice in the Nineties*, eds. Kathleen Hughes, R.S.C.J. and Mark R. Francis, C.S.V. (Collegeville, Minnesota: The Liturgical Press, 1991), 154–155.

13. Wadell, "What Do All Those Masses Do For Us?," 154–155.

14. Lathrop, *Holy People*, 88.

15. Lathrop, *Holy People*, 166–167.

16. World Council of Churches, *One Baptism, One Eucharist and a Mutually Recognized Ministry* (Geneva, Switzerland, 1978), 23 (#'s 21–23).

17. R. Kevin Seasoltz, O.S.B., "Liturgy and Social Consciousness," 54.

18. R. Kevin Seasoltz, O.S.B., "The Sacred Liturgy: Development and Directions" in *Remembering the Future: Vatican II and Tomorrow's Liturgical Agenda*, ed. Carl A. Last (New York: Paulist Press, 1983), 48.

19. James L. Empereur, S.J., and Christopher G. Kiesling, O.P., *The Liturgy That Does Justice* (Collegeville, Minnesota: The Liturgical Press, 1990), 15.

20. Regis Duffy, O.F.M., *Real Presence: Worship, Sacraments and Commitment* (San Francisco: Harper and Row, 1982), 3.

21. Robert L. Kinast, *Caring for Society: A Theological Interpretation of Lay Ministry* (Chicago: The Thomas More Press, 1985), 96.

22. Duffy, *Real Presence*, 23.

23. Hans Bernhard Meyer, "The Social Significance of the Liturgy" in *Politics and Liturgy*, eds. Herman Schmidt and David Power (New York: Herder and Herder, 1974), 37.

24. Lathrop, *Holy People*, 45.

25. Lathrop, *Holy People*, 32–33.

26. Lathrop, *Holy People*, 59–65. Also See I Corinthians 8, 10, 12 and 14.

27. Lathrop, *Holy People*, 166.

28. Lathrop, *Holy People*, 104.

29. Lathrop, *Holy People*, 56.

30. Dianne Bergant, C.S.A., "Liturgy and Scripture: Creating a New World" in *Liturgy and Social Justice: Celebrating Rites—Proclaiming Rights*, ed. Edward M. Grosz.(Collegeville, Minnesota: The Liturgical Press, 1989), 12.

31. See *Lumen Gentium* #'s and 31, *Ad Gentes Divinitus* #15 and *Gaudium et Spes* #'s 40–42.

32. See *Sacrosanctum Concilium* #10, *Lumen Gentium* #'s 8, 17, 31, 33, 36, 40–42 and *Gaudium et Spes* #'s 40–42.

33. Jerome Kodell, O.S.B., *The Eucharist in the New Testament* (Collegeville, Minnesota: The Liturgical Press, 1988), 38–52. See also Gary Macy, *The Banquet's Wisdom: A Short History of the Theologies of the Lord's Supper* (New York: Paulist Press, 1992), 16.

34. Jerome Murphy-O'Connor, "Eucharist and Community in First Corinthians" in *Living Bread, Living Cup*, ed. R. Kevin Seasoltz, O.S.B. (Collegeville, Minnesota: The Liturgical Press, 1987), 17. See also I Corinthians 6:15, 11:27–29 and 12:12.

35. Murphy-O'Connor, *Eucharist and Community*, 20–21. See also I Corinthians 10:17 and 11:26–28.

36. Murphy-O'Connor, *Eucharist and Community*, 21. See also Macy, *The Banquet's Wisdom*, 29.

37. Kodell, *The Eucharist in the New Testament*, 91. See also Keenan B. Osborne, O.F.M., *The Christian Sacraments of Initiation: Baptism, Confirmation, Eucharist* (New York: Paulist Press, 1987), 143–233.

38. Kodell, *The Eucharist in the New Testament*, 110; 115–116.

39. Kodell, *The Eucharist in the New Testament*,63 and Macy, *Banquet's Wisdom*, 23.

40. Macy, *Banquet's Wisdom*, 53.

41. Daniel J. Sheerin, *Message of the Fathers of the Church: The Eucharist* (Wilmington, Delaware: Michael Glazier, 1986), 34–35. See also Macy, *Banquet's Wisdom*, 20 and 28.

42. Sheerin, *Message of the Fathers*, 212–215.

43. Sheerin, *Message of the Fathers*, 285–287.

44. Sheerin, *Message of the Fathers*, 220.

45. Ralph A. Keifer, "Liturgy and Ethics: Some Unresolved Dilemmas" in *Living No Longer for Ourselves: Liturgy and Justice in the Nineties*, eds. Kathleen Hughes, R.S.C.J. and Mark R. Francis, C.S.V. (Collegeville, Minnesota: The Liturgical Press, 1991), 73.

46. Keifer, "Liturgy and Ethics," 73

47. Macy, *Banquet's Wisdom*, 131.

48. See St. Thomas Aquinas, *Summa Theologica* (Q. 82 Art. 1; Q. 74 Arts.1–8; Q. 75 Art. 2 to Q. 78 Art. 6).

49. Macy, *Banquet's Wisdom*, 175f.

50. See Kodell, *The Eucharist in the New Testament*, and Macy, *Banquet's Wisdom*, 15f.

51. Gustavo Gutierrez, *A Theology of Liberation* (Maryknoll, New York: Orbis Books, 1995), 147.

Chapter Three

Ministry and Mission of Service of the People of God

THE CENTRAL ROLE OF THE LAITY
IN THE CHURCH OF THE TWENTY FIRST CENTURY

The very titles, as well as content, of Vatican II's two principle documents pertaining directly to ecclesiology, *Lumen Gentium* and *Gaudium et Spes,* bespeak the Church's conviction that as a sacrament she is to reveal the Light, Joy and Hope of Humanity, i.e., Jesus Christ, to the world. At the heart of the Council's vision and ecclesiological directives was an emphasis on the pastoral nature of the Church—the conviction that theology must unfold into ministry at the service of all: "The pilgrim church is missionary by her very nature" *(Ad Gentes Divinitus #2)*. Acknowledging that the missionary task of the Church is inherently one of perpetuating and extending the saving activity of Christ, the Council posited the Church's missionary outreach, like Christ's, must be universal in scope and addressed to all persons. This universal task necessitates that all members of the Church participate in Her mission of service. Empowered by the charisms of baptism and the grace of the Eucharist, the laity have a particularly important role to play in the Church's universal mission. The laity are the Church's primary point of contact with the plethora of historical and cultural experiences which mark the Church. Consequently, the laity are in position to discern the "signs of the times" that mark the modern world and to inform the Church's efforts of *aggiornamento* and inculturation. Pope John Paul II stated:

> A new state of affairs today both in the Church and in the social, economic, political and cultural life, calls with particular urgency for the action of the lay faithful . . . It is not permissible for anyone to remain idle *(Christifideles Laici #3)*.

The lay faithful have an essential and irreplaceable role...through them the
Church of Christ is made present in the various sectors of the world as a sign
and source of hope and of love (*Christifideles Laici #7*).

THE CHURCH IS THE PEOPLE OF GOD
DEDICATED TO THE KINGDOM

The Second Vatican Council's Dogmatic Constitution on the Church, *Lumen
Gentium,* defines the Church as the People of God prior to considering the
Church in Her hierarchical and religious dimensions. Such priority recognizes
that the call of salvation is a communal phenomenon. Salvation History reveals
to us that God saves His chosen as a people, and that He utilizes His Chosen
People as an instrument through which He reveals Himself to others. This is ac-
complished when the chosen community lives in a manner which reveals God
to others. As the people of the New Covenant, all members of the church have
a role to play in extending God's saving invitation to all persons. The Church
is a community entrusted with the task of communicating God's saving deeds
and call to salvation to all people. Consequently the church must enter into all
dimensions of human life to proclaim these truths. As the People of God:

> . . . the Church is destined to extend to all regions of the earth and so must en-
> ter into the history of humankind (*Lumen Gentium #9*) . . . for all humanity is
> called to belong to the new people of God . . . (*Lumen Gentium #13*).

In short,

> . . . the Church is compelled by the Holy Spirit to do her part so that God's plan
> may be fully realized . . . She prepares Her hearers to receive and profess the
> faith . . . the obligation of spreading the faith is imposed upon every disciple of
> Christ (*Lumen Gentium #17*).

From this perspective, the Council views the Church to be all disciples of
Christ presenting themselves to God for the sake of bearing witness to Christ
and providing an answer to those who hope for and seek eternal life (*Lumen
Gentium #10*). George Lindbeck has noted that this vision of church affirms
the church as the people of God and clarifies her mission as one of service
unto others:

> Because the function of the Church in all aspects of its life and action is to point
> to the Kingdom of love and justice which has come and is coming, its concrete
> service to humankind is no less integral a part of its mission and its witness than
> are its preaching, worship and communal life.[1]

Key to Vatican II's ecclesiology is a sense of mission devoted to serving the modern world primarily through the laity and their communal service unto the world.[2] Such a vision accentuates the historical existential nature of the church as it downplays excessive institutionalism and emphasizes God's activity in human communities.

Such a vision of Church and its corresponding mission reveals the Incarntional mentality which colors the Council's ecclesiology. Tempering notions of distant eschatology, an Incarnational model suggests that human actions contribute to the preparation for the Kingdom of God. This emphasis, again, accentuates the role of laity, for it is the laity who reside within all the varying cultures, serving as the link between the Church and the world.

Jon Sobrino recognizes in this focus on the Church as People of God and their mission of service a possible means of easing the split between Classical Essentialism and Historical Existentialism, for it challenges the Church to be a historical manifestation of God's love for the world. The focus on temporal renewal in anticipation of the Kingdom of God serves to unify the transcendent values of God with the efforts of social justice facilitated by the Church:

> In this Kingdom of God history and transcendence are unified. The Kingdom must be a historical entity, and it is through and not apart from this historical entity, as well as through and not apart from human beings, that the way is prepared for the eschatological fulfillment which, as fulfillment, is no longer human work but God's. The vertical and horizontal dimensions of Christian existence are also brought into unity in the Kingdom. Unified too are two aspects of the human person—seeker of meaning and maker of meaning. In Christian terms, human beings as seekers of meaning find it by allowing God to communicate with them; as makers of meaning they create it by building the Kingdom of God. The problem of the relationship between faith and justice must be approached from the starting point of this unity that both unifies and is itself unified. In the interaction of building the Kingdom and building it according to the will of God, faith and justice are brought into the course of history.[3]

So critical are the interconnections between the Church's faith and Her ministry of social service that the Council Fathers sternly warned:

> One of the gravest errors of our time is the dichotomy between faith which many profess and the practice of their daily lives. As far back as the Old Testament the prophets vehemently denounced this scandal, and in the New Testament Christ, Himself, with greater force threatens it with severe punishment. Let there, then, be no such pernicious opposition between professional and social activity on the one hand and religious life on the other. The Christian who shirks his temporal duties shirks his duties towards his neighbor, neglects God Himself, and endangers his

eternal salvation . . . It is to the laity . . . that secular duties and activity properly belong . . . It is their task to cultivate a properly informed conscience and to impress the divine law on the affairs of the earthly city . . . The laity are called to participate actively in the whole life of the Church; not only are they to animate the world with the Spirit of Christianity, but they are to be witness to Christ in all circumstances and at the very heart of the community of humankind (*Gaudium et Spes, #43*).

THE KINGLY DIMENSION OF BAPTISMAL DIGNITY AND THE LAY APOSTOLATE

As we have seen in the preceding Chapters, Vatican II moved toward greater lay/cleric equality within the life and ministries of the Church when the Council affirmed that all baptized Christians share in the priestly, prophetic and kingly ministries of Jesus. Such an emphasis is unprecedented and a notable move away from the then prevailing perception of the laity as passive recipients of ecclesial works, and of the lay apostolate as a subordinate and secondary apostolate to that of the hierarchy. Flowing from their baptismal dignity, laity have the "noble duty of working to extend the divine plan of salvation to all humans of each epoch and in every land" (*Lumen Gentium #33*). Such affirmation of the dignity and responsibilities of the laity had tremendous effects upon the future of the lay apostolate.

Vatican II maintained that "the lay apostolate is a participation in the salvific mission of the Church itself" (*Lumen Gentium #33*). The lay apostolate does not derive from, nor is it enabled by participation in the apostolate of the hierarchy. The lay apostolate is a right, duty and obligation of the laity as baptized members of the Church and co-sharers of the Church's salvific mission—it is an apostolate in its own right with its own validity and its own innate legitimacy. The lay apostolate is specifically a mission of ministry in the midst of and unto the world:

> The laity by their very vocation seek the Kingdom of God by engaging in temporal affairs and by ordering them according to the plan of God. They live in the world, that is, in each and in all of the secular professions and occupations. They live in ordinary circumstances of family and social life, from which the very web of their existence is woven. They are called their by God that by exercising their proper function and led by the Spirit of the Gospel they may work for the sanctification of the world from within as a leaven. In this way they make Christ known to others . . . (*Lumen Gentium #31*).

(The lay apostolate) is exercised when they (the laity) work at the evangelization and sanctification of humanity; it is exercised, too, when they endeavor to have the Gospel Spirit permeate and improve the temporal order, going about it in a way that bears witness to Christ and helps forward the salvation of humanity. The characteristic of the lay state being a life in the midst of the world and of secular affairs, the laity are called by God to make of their apostolate, through the vigor of their Christian Spirit, a leaven in the world (*Apostolicam Actuositatem* #2).

It is clear that the vision of the Church as the sacrament of the Paschal Mystery characterized by a mission and ministry of service unto the world involves the laity in the renewal of the temporal order.

The work of Christ's redemption concerns essentially the salvation of humanity; it takes in also, however, the renewal of the whole temporal order. The mission of the Church, consequently, is not only to bring people the message of grace and of Christ, but also to permeate and improve the whole range of the temporal. The laity, carrying out this mission of the Church, exercise their apostolate therefore in the world . . . (*Apostolicam Actuositatem* #5).

This mission is realized via the historical-existential living out the example of Christ in the daily lives of the faithful. If the Church is to be successful, then we, the faithful, must give evidence of Christ in every dimension of our lives.

The Church is not truly established and does not fully live, nor is a perfect sign of Christ unless there is a genuine laity existing and working alongside the hierarchy. For the Gospel cannot become deeply rooted in the mentality, life and work of people without the active presence of lay people (*Ad Gentes Divinitus* #21).

In short, the Church cannot serve as a sacrament of Christ to the world unless her members live their lives in such a way to reveal Christ to others. Acting as sacraments themselves, the faithful enable the Church to act as a sacrament. The awesome responsibility that this vision and self-understanding of what it means to be Church bestows upon the laity cannot be overstated. We laity must respond to the challenge bestowed upon us by the Holy Spirit and live our lives within and outside of the Church in a manner that both reveals Christ, and claims as our own our rightful role in the Church's mission to the world and her own *ad intra* experiences as community.

THE KINGLY DIMENSION OF BAPTISMAL DIGNITY AND ECCLESIAL AUTHORITY

As sharers in the kingly dignity of Christ via Baptism, the lay members of the church not only are entrusted with the impregnation of the temporal realm with the Spirit of the Gospel and the transformation of the secular order in anticipation of the Kingdom of God, the laity also have a right to participate in the authoritative decision-making processes of the Church, herself. Vatican II recovered the New Testament teaching of ministry as *diakonia*—a ministry of service shared by and at the service of the entire community.[4] The New Testament describes the ecclesial community as *koinonia,* i.e., relationships based upon mutuality and reciprocity, sharing, communication, and equality in giving and receiving.[5] This image of church as communion is one that is asserted 127 times in Pope John Paul II's *Christfideles Laici,* and a concept which echoes the image of the church as the Body of Christ. Both images recognize a diversity of persons/gifts intimately drawn together in relationships of interdependence, reciprocity, mutuality and shared life efforts toward the common good.[6] When these visions of church are linked with the baptismal dignity of all members of the ecclesial community and the co-discipleship to which all the baptized are united, and the shared Spirit which all of the baptized experience, it is clear to see that baptism endows all members of the church with a shared ministry and mission of authority. This is captured in Vatican II's call for ecclesial collegiality.[7]

The ecclesiological implications that a renewed appreciation for the threefold dignity of baptism and the social dimensions of the Eucharist have yet to be fully explored. These emphases, along with the Church's commitment to be the sacrament of the Paschal Mystery unto the world, will demand increased involvement of the laity in all dimensions of ecclesial life. As the Church sojourns as a pilgrim journeying through the twenty first century, she will have to increasingly turn to her lay members to discern how she can best address, speak to and shed the light of the Gospel upon the lived experience of all persons in a manner that is intelligible, meaningful, viable and readily assimilated.

As a result of these ecclesial developments, William J. Rademacher and Hans Kung have called for partnership and shared ministry in the authoritative teaching process which governs the Church—a call which we believe is indispensable to the Church of the twenty first century as it strives to be faithful to what the Spirit is saying and to be at the service of all persons. In the decades after the Second Vatican Council there has been a call for consultative ecclesial bodies—a call which suggests that shared ministry involves shared dialogue, planning and policy-making.[8]

> As members (of the Church), they (the laity) share a common dignity from their rebirth in Christ. They have the same filial grace and the same vocation to perfection . . . Hence, there is in Christ and in the Church no inequality . . . If therefore everyone in the Church does not proceed by the same path, nevertheless all are called to sanctity and have received an equal privilege of faith through the justice of God . . . all share a true equality with regard to the dignity and to the activity common to all the faithful for building up the Body of Christ. For the

distinction which the Lord made between sacred ministers and the rest of the people of God entails a unifying purpose, since pastors and the other faithful are bound to each other by mutual need (*Lumen Gentium #2*).

Let sacred pastors recognize and promote the dignity as well as the responsibility of the laity in the Church. Let them willingly make use of their prudent advice. Let them confidently assign duties to them in the service of the Church, allowing them freedom and room for action. Further, let them encourage the laity so that they may undertake this task on their own initiative . . . In this way, the whole Church, strengthened by each one of its members, can more effectively fulfill its mission for the life of the world (*Lumen Gentium #37*).

Priests are to be sincere in their appreciation of and promotion of lay people's dignity and of the special role the laity have to play in the Church's mission . . . They should be willing to listen to lay people, give brotherly consideration to their wishes, and recognize their experience and competence in the different fields of human activity. In this way, they will be able to recognize along with them the signs of the times (*Presbyterorum Ordinis #9*).

In order to be able to provide for the welfare of the faithful as their individual circumstance demand, he (the bishop) should try to keep himself informed of their needs . . . To this end he should employ suitable methods . . . He should be solicitous of all persons . . . In exercising his ministry he should recognize their right and duty to play their part in building up the Mystical Body of Christ (*Christus Dominus #16*).

Of course, such a model of ministry is advocated by Christ, Himself:

You know that among the pagans their so-called rulers lord it over them, and their great men make their authority felt. This is not to happen among you. No; anyone who wants to become great among you must be your servant, and anyone who wants to be first among you must be slave to all. For the Son of Man Himself did not come to be served but to serve, and to give His life as ransom for many (Mark 10:42–45).

Vatican II shifted the ecclesiological focus from the universal church to the local church, recognizing that each assembly of the church is a creation of the Holy Spirit, visibly representing the entire ecclesial community via its love, Eucharistic life, vocations, and adherence to the will of God, example of Jesus and prompting of the Holy Spirit:

This church of Christ is truly present in all legitimate local congregations of the faithful . . . For in their locality these are the new people called by God, in the Holy Spirit . . . In these communities . . . Christ is present. By His power, the one, holy, catholic and apostolic church is gathered together (*Lumen Gentium #26*).

Within each individual church there exist the one unique Catholic Church
. . . This variety of local churches . . . demonstrates with greater clarity the
catholicity of the . . . church (*Lumen Gentium* #23).

Given these ecclesial developments, the questions and musings of Hans
Kung are deeply relevant:

People like to talk of the participation of the laity in the life of the Church. They
also like to speak of the participation of the laity in the decisions of the world.
They do not at all like to speak, at least in official binding documents, of the participation of the laity in the decisions of the Church.[9]

. . . if the laity are to be included as advisors and collaborators, then why not
also as decision makers?[10]

If from a biblical perspective the shepherds are not the masters but the servants
of the Church or congregation (laity), why then should it in practice be possible
to exclude the Church or congregation from joint decision-making?[11]

Kung points out a troubling phenomenon which will have to be overcome if the
Church is to be a vital community in the twenty first century—the effects of cler-
icalism and the ontological distinction of the clergy which accompanies Orders
in the Classical Essentialistic view continue to have a hold on the Church's
praxis despite Vatican II's efforts to overcome them. As Kung argues, to
contribute to the advice and work of the Church, only to be excluded from its
decision-making, continues to render the laity second-class members of the ecclesial community.[12] Both the dignity of the laity by virtue of baptism, and the
nature of the leadership of servant-hood that is to characterize the clergy, demand that collaboration become the model of ecclesial decision-making.

So the shepherds and the congregation have their mutual obligations: the shepherds have the duty and the task to proclaim the Christian message to the congregation . . . even when it is uncomfortable for the congregation. The congregation, on the other hand, has the duty and the task of retesting again and again
whether the shepherds are remaining true to their commission, whether they are
acting according to the gospel.[13]

However, for this collaboration to be meaningful, and for it to respect the dignity of the laity, it will have to be authoritative in a sense with real integrity,
authenticity, and power, i.e., it must be embodied structurally and institution-
ally in meaningful ways, carrying magisterial clout.

As we see it, such attentiveness to the ministry of authority of the laity is
precisely attentiveness to what the Spirit is saying to the churches of the
twenty first century. Such attentiveness to the Spirit is what Pope John Paul
II identified as the primary task of the Church in the new millennium.[14] In
Tertio Millennio Adveniente, Pope John Paul II described the Church's renewed attention to the Spirit's working within the laity as being: . . .

aimed at an increased sensitivity to all that the Spirit is saying to the Church and to the Churches, as well as to individuals through charisms meant to serve the whole community. The purpose is to emphasize what the Spirit is suggesting to different communities, from smallest ones . . . taking into account cultures, societies and sound traditions (*Tertio Millennio Adveniente* #23).

The Pope, like Kung, suggested that this attentiveness to the laity inspired by the Second Vatican Council is only in its infancy and awaits greater expression and institutional recognition as the Church journeys into the new millennium in the midst of the New Advent begun at Vatican II, waiting to see how and where the Spirit will speak, and to whom, as the Lord ever guides the Church on her journey in and through each and all of her members. As stated before, such guidance of the Spirit would only be accentuated if the prophetic role within the Church was identified, affirmed, utilized and able to act as the Pneumatic corrective it is intended to be. We must recall from Scripture that the voice of the prophet was the voice of authority within the community of faith, for the prophet was inspired by God's Spirit and spoke His Word to the people—all people, even the king!

THE SACRAMENTS AND THE LAY APOSTOLATE

If the laity are to be successful in their efforts to live the Christ-like life in the midst of the world and discern what the Spirit is saying to the church so that they can share in the decision-making process of the Church, they will need to be empowered, nourished and sustained by the sacraments. We have already explored how the sacraments of baptism (See Chapter 1 and above) and the Eucharist (See Chapter 2) facilitate these ends. Let us now examine how the sacraments of confirmation and marriage also enable the laity in their mission and ministry of service unto the world on behalf of the Church.

CONFIRMATION:
THE SACRAMENT OF THE LAY APOSTOLATE

As was briefly alluded to in Chapter One, the Church has always understood the unique charism of the sacrament of confirmation to be a gift of the Holy Spirit which strengthens the recipient to give public witness to their faith and to actively contribute to the building up (be "soldiers" of Christ) of the Church and the Kingdom of God. Vatican II reaffirmed this understanding of confirmation's peculiar charism:

> By the sacrament of confirmation the faithful are more perfectly bound to the Church and are endowed with the special strength of the Holy Spirit. Hence they

are, as true witnesses of Christ, more strictly obliged to spread the faith by word and deed (*Lumen Gentium* #11).

Strengthened by the power of the Holy Spirit in the sacrament of confirmation, it is by the Lord, Himself, that one is assigned to the lay apostolate . . . In order that one may in all one's actions bear witness to Christ all the world over . . . On all Christians, accordingly, rests the noble obligation of working to bring all persons throughout the world to hear and to accept the divine message of salvation (*Apostolicam Actuositatem* #3).

If one examines the theological history and emphasis of the sacrament of confirmation throughout the Church's tradition, and compares it to the lay apostolate as articulated by the Second Vatican Council, one will discover that both, confirmation and the lay apostolate, share the same theological trajectories and emphases. Consequently, one of the challenges the Church of the twenty first century faces is the challenge of better articulating the interconnection which exists between the lay apostolate and the sacrament of confirmation. This will enable the confirmed to have a better appreciation for their roles and responsibilities in the building up of the Church as well as their contribution to society's advancement toward the Kingdom of God. If the transformation of the temporal order and the corrective voice of the Holy Spirit within the Church are functions and tasks facilitated by the Holy Spirit, then the sacrament of confirmation must be connected to both in some way, for its specific grace is a profound grace of the Holy Spirit intended for a public purpose. In addition to baptism, then, the sacramental dignity which confirmation bestows upon the recipient enables them to share in the priestly, prophetic and kingly ministries of Christ, both vis-a-vis the world and within the Church.

MARRIED AND FAMILY LIFE AS THE DOMESTIC AND VITAL CELL OF SOCIETY

Married life, too, is identified by the Council as having signific vis-a-vis the Church's apostolate of service to the world an serve as a sacrament of Christ's Paschal Mystery. The very c ment dedicated to articulating the Council's vision of the Chur the world, *Gaudium et Spes*, only treats one sacrament at leng ment of marriage. This emphasis evidences the bishops' convic riage and family life are indispensable to the Church's missio and efficacy in acting as a sacrament of Christ.

Pope John Paul II, in *Familiaris Consortio*, beautifully expou vision of family life. The Pope affirmed the Council's vision of family life as revealing God's covenant with humanity, Jesus' emptying) and *agapic* (unconditional) love, and its ability to serve as an example to others, inspiring them to such community and love. Pope John Paul II noted that marriage and family life are indispensable to the efforts to create communities, serve life, develop society, and, thus, share in the life and mission of the Church.

Describing married life as a community of life and love, the Council Fathers recognized that marriage and family life are in miniature what the entire church is called to be, i.e., a sacrament of the Paschal Mystery to the world. The mutual giving of self to the other in the exchange of love between the spouses, and the incessant service parents render unto children, serve to reveal to the world (and to the wider Church) the example of Christ's *kenotic* love.

Since marriage and family life is lived in the midst of the world, it has the power to communicate this divine reality to others and, consequently, the power to draw others to know and experience God's great love for humanity.[15]

> The family, because it arises from marriage, which is an image of the covenant of love of Christ and the Church, and a participation in this covenant, will disclose to all the living presence of the Savior in the world, as well as show also the authentic nature of the Church (*Gaudium et Spes* #48).

> Married persons, themselves . . . will bear witness, by their faithful love in the joys and sacrifices of their calling, to that mystery of love which the Lord revealed to the world by His death and Resurrection (*Gaudium et Spes* #52).

Its ability to convey the truth of the Paschal Mystery intimately links married life to the wellbeing of the church and society:

> The apostolate of married persons and of families has a special importance for both the church and civil society (*Apostolicam Actuositatem* #11).

> The well being of the individual person and of both human and Christian society is closely bound up with the healthy state of conjugal and family life (*Gaudium et Spes* #47).

> The Christian family constitutes a specific revelation and realization of ecclesial communion, and for this reason too it can and should be called the domestic church (*Familiaris Consortio* #21).

Here we see the conviction that married and family life are a unique expression of the lay apostolate which facilitates the Church's ministry and mission of service, for they evidence covenantal, *kenotic* and communal love, and serve to inform others regarding what is needed to create bonds of solidarity and service to others.[16]

> The mission of being the primary vital cell of society has been given to the family by God Himself. This mission will be accomplished if the family . . . offers

active hospitality and practices justice and other good works for the benefit of others . . . Christian families bear a very valuable witness to Christ before the world when all their life they remain attached to the Gospel and hold up the example of Christian marriage (*Apostolicam Actuositatem* #11).

Married and family life succeed in serving this role for the Church and world when they incarnate in their daily life and activities the ideals of love, reconciliation, justice, peace, hospitality, equal dignity, mutual reciprocity, etc., and when they teach the skills of creating community, communicating and listening, sharing, etc.—the very ideals and tasks which are to mark the Church's missionary apostolate of service to the world.[17]

The family is the first school of those social virtues which every society needs . . . It is through the family that children are gradually introduced into civic partnership with their fellow human beings . . . (*Gravitisimus Educationis* #3).

The family is the first and fundamental school of social living . . . The self-giving which inspires the love of husband and wife for each other is the model and norm for the self- giving that must be practiced in (all) relationships . . . And the communion and sharing that are part of everyday life in the home . . . are the most concrete and effective pedagogy for the active, responsible and fruitful inclusion of children in the wider horizon of society (*Familiaris Consortio* #37).

It is from the family that citizens come to birth and it is within the family that they find the first school of the social virtues that are the animating principle of the existence and development of society itself . . . The very experience of communion and sharing that should characterize the family's daily life represents its first and fundamental contribution to society . . . Thus the fostering of authentic and mature communion between persons within the family is the first and irreplaceable school of social life, and example and stimulus for the broader community of relationships marked by respect, justice, dialogue and love. The family is thus . . . the place of origin and the most effective means for humanizing and personalizing society . . . (*Familaris Consortio* #'s 42–43).

Additionally, the Church would benefit pastorally if it were to adopt a more familial model of institutional organization, structure and means of exercising authority. As we have seen, marriage and family life encapsulate in miniature the ministerial ideal of service and model of communion that are to be marks of the Church. As the Church of the twenty first century seeks to implement structural and institutional changes to enable collaborative, partnered and shared decision-making among all persons within the Church, family life can and should serve as a model of inspiration. Familial relations move beyond self-interest to the edification of the family as a whole. Familial relationships build community by incorporating individual members into a wider group. A familial model would move beyond the institutional model which predominates now by focusing members of the Church on one another, allowing for a greater depth of interpersonal relations. Such relations would arouse greater acknowledgment of the mutual responsibilities that each member has for one another and remind us of the obligations we have to the larger group.[18]

PARTICIPATION, DEMOCRATIZATION AND THE PRINCIPLE OF SOLIDARITY

This model of shared responsibility, decision-making and authority which is characteristic of healthy family life and ought to mark the Church of the twenty first century is consistent with the magisterial teachings of recent decades—teachings which have defined participation and equality as basic forms of human dignity and freedom; have consistently identified participation in governance as a fundamental human right; which have acknowledged democratic forms of decision-making most consistent with human nature; and that have cited that the practice of subsidiarity ought to be a guiding principle in all collegial efforts. Furthermore, the very integrity of the Church demands that such principles, which she expects and demands of other institutions, be embraced and applied to her very self. Double standards and hypocrisy have no room in the Church of the twenty first century.

> . . . two aspirations persistently make themselves felt in these new contexts, and they grow stronger to the extent that people become informed and better educated: the aspiration to equality and the aspiration to participation, two forms of human dignity and freedom (*Octogesima Adveniens* #22).

> . . . a demand made by the people of today: a greater sharing in responsibility and in decision-making. This legitimate aspiration becomes more evident as the cultural level rises, as the sense of freedom develops and as persons become more aware of how, in a world facing an uncertain future, the choices of today already condition the world of tomorrow . . . modern forms of democracy must be devised, not only making it possible for each person to become informed and to express oneself, but also involving them in a shared responsibility (*Octogesima Adveniens* #47).

> It is in full accord with human nature that juridical-political structures should, with ever better success and without any discrimination, afford all their citizens the chance to participate freely and actively in establishing the constitutional bases of political community, governing the state, determining the scope and purpose of various institutions, and choosing leaders (*Gaudium et Spes* #75).

Citizens, for their part, should remember that they have the right and duty, which must be recognized by civil authority, to contribute according to their ability to the true progress of their own community (*Gaudium et Spes* #65).

The Church values the democratic system inasmuch as it ensures the participation of citizens in making political choices, guarantees to the governed the possibility of both electing and holding accountable those who govern them, and of replacing them through peaceful means when appropriate (*Centesimus Annus* #46).

The principle of subsidiarity must be respected: a community of a higher order should not interfere in the internal life of a community of a lower order, depriving the latter of its functions, but rather should support it in case of need and help to coordinate its activity with the activities of the rest of society, always with a view to the common good (*Centesimus Annus* #48).

These principles and ideals are binding not only upon civic entities and secular organizations, but on the Church as well. This is because they are rooted in human dignity, and in humanity's social and relational nature. Unless the Church demonstrates the courage to adapt these principles to her own structures and institutional mechanisms of power, then her advocacy of human dignity and call for solidarity will all be rendered void of credibility. Above all, if the Church is to serve as the sacrament of the Paschal Mystery of Christ, then she must evidence the veracity of her teachings first and foremost in her own example!

Embodying these principles and ideals in her own example, and allowing for the laity to share in the authority of the Church in a meaningful way, will require a tremendous act of *kenosis* on the part of the Church. Her structural, institutional and magisterial mechanisms will have to empty themselves of their clerical dominance and introduce ways for the laity to participate in meaningful ways, with equal dignity and shared authority and decision-making powers. The laity, in turn, will have to empty themselves of their own subjective needs and wants and exercise their authority in a manner that is edifying to the entire ecclesial community and in agreement with the clergy. Both laity and clergy must evidence the courage and conviction in the very reality they seek to communicate—the Paschal Mystery and its revelation that out of such *kenosis* new life will come to the Church as the Holy Spirit leads us. The Church's failure to reform herself according to the very principles and ideals which she, herself, cites as best for communal life, will spell her demise in the twenty first century:

It cannot be forgotten that the manner in which the individual exercises their freedom is conditioned in innumerable ways. While these certainly have an influence on freedom, they do not determine it; they make the exercise of freedom more difficult or less difficult, but they cannot destroy it. Not only is it wrong from the ethical point of view to disregard human nature, which is made for freedom, but in practice it is impossible to do so. Where society is so organized as to reduce arbitrarily or even suppress the sphere in which freedom is legitimately exercised, the result is that the life of society becomes progressively disorganized and goes into decline (*Centesimus Annus* #25).

Only if clergy and laity alike share and maintain a focus on the common good will the Church persevere as a communion at the service of others, revealing Christ to all.

NOTES

1. George A. Lindbeck, *The Future of Roman Catholic Theology* (Philadelphia: Fortress Press, 1962), 38.

2. Lindbeck, *The Future of Roman Catholic Theology*, 27–37.

3. Jon Sobrino, *The True Church and The Poor* (Maryknoll, New York: Orbis Books, 1984), 73.

4. William J. Rademacher, *Lay Ministry: A Theological, Spiritual and Pastoral Handbook* (New York: Crossroad, 1992), 169.

5. Rademacher, *Lay Ministry*, 170.

6. Rademacher, *Lay Ministry*, 171–172.

7. Rademacher, *Lay Ministry*, 172–174.

8. Rademacher, *Lay Ministry*, 176.

9. Hans Kung, *Reforming the Church Today: Keeping Hope Alive* (Crossroad: New York, 1990.), 75.

10. Kung, *Reforming the Church Today*, 79.

11. Kung, *Reforming the Church Today*, 83.

12. Kung, *Reforming the Church Today*, 75.

13. Kung, *Reforming the Church Today*, 86.

14. See Pope John Paul II, *Tertio Millennio Adveniente* #'s 44–46.

15. See Joann Heaney Hunter, "Domestic Church: Guiding Beliefs and Daily Practices," "Living the Baptismal Commitment in Sacramental Marriage" and William P. Roberts, "The Family as Domestic Church: Contemporary Implications" in *Christian Marriage and Family-Contemporary Theological and Pastoral Perspectives*, eds. Michael G. Lawler and William P. Roberts (Collegeville, Minnesota: The Liturgical Press, 1996).

16. Ibid.

17. Ibid.

18. John H. Westerhoff, *Living The Faith Community: The Church That Makes A Difference* (Minneapolis, Minnesota: Winston Press, 1985), 78–83.

Chapter Four

The Church: Ministry and Mission of Servant-Leaders

INTRODUCTION

In 1995, thirty years after the end of the Second Vatican Council, Pope John Paul II issued his encyclical on the Church's commitment to ecumenism, *Ut Unum Sint*. The unity of Christians had been a significant theme of the Council and important ecumenical dialogues had taken place subsequently over the intervening years between Roman Catholics and other Christians. In 1991 the Congregation for the Doctrine of the Faith (CDF) offered its response to the *Final Report* of the first Anglican-Roman Catholic International Commission (ARCIC-I) which had worked from 1969–1981 formulating statements on *Eucharistic Doctrine* (1971), *Ministry and Ordination* (1973) and *Authority in the Church I* (1976). The response of the CDF indicated that it was not yet possible to state that substantial agreement on the questions which the Commission had considered had been reached. The CDF asked for further clarifications of the areas of agreement presented in the report. In early September 1993 the second Anglican-Roman Catholic International Commission (ARCIC - II) sent to the Vatican a paper entitled *Clarifications of Certain Aspects of the Agreed Statements on Eucharist and Ministry*. Cardinal Edward Cassidy, President of the Pontifical Council for Promoting Christian Unity, responded in March 1994:

> I am now in a position to assure you that the said clarifications have indeed thrown new light on the questions concerning Eucharist and ministry in the Final Report of ARCIC-I for which further study had been requested. The Pontifical Council for Promoting Christian Unity is therefore most grateful to the members of ARCIC-II and ARCIC-I who prepared these clarifications. The agreement reached on Eucharist and ministry by ARCIC-I is thus greatly strengthened, and no further study would seem to be required at this stage.[1]

The Anglican-Roman Catholic dialogue on the doctrine of the Eucharist, ministry and ordination and authority in the Church between 1969 and 1994 formed an important part of the background for Pope John Paul's understanding of his ministry of service to the Church presented in *Ut Unum Sint.*

Taught by the events of her history, the church is committed to freeing herself from every purely human support in order to live in depth the Gospel law of the Beatitudes. Conscious that the truth does not impose itself except "by virtue of its own truth, as it makes its entrance into the mind at once quietly and with power," she seeks nothing for herself but the freedom to proclaim the Gospel. Indeed, her authority is exercised in the service of truth and charity.[2]

The long years of the Anglican-Roman Catholic dialogue and *Ut Unum Sint* provide an excellent horizon for asking ourselves: what is the Spirit saying to the Churches in the following areas: 1) the ministry and mission of servant leaders; 2) the Bishop of Rome as the servant of the servants of God unto unity and diversity and 3) the authority of the people of God, theologians, and the bishops and the Pope in Council? We shall discuss servant leaders in this chapter; the ministry of the Bishop of Rome in Chapter 5, and the question of authority in Chapter 6.

THE CHALLENGE OF A NEW APPROPRIATION
OF THE CHRISTIAN DICHOTOMIES

In the statement quoted above from *Ut Unum Sint,* Pope John Paul says that "taught by the events of her history, the church is committed to freeing herself from every purely human support in order to live in depth the Gospel law of the Beatitudes." This very important statement opens up the crucial question of the ongoing struggle between an essentialist and an existentialist vision of the Church that is present in all the documents of Vatican II and in the subsequent implementation of that vision during the past forty years. The essentialist and existentialist visions of the Church are a contemporary example of the dichotomies that mark all aspects of the Christian faith. From the essentialist perspective, the Church and its teachings, in their very essence, are beyond the ever changing world of transient structures and thought forms that mark diverse cultures through which the Church has lived for centuries. In the essentialist vision of the Church that we find in the First Vatican Council (1869–1870), the magisterium holds central place and theology's role is to explain revealed truths that have been defined; to defend orthodox doctrines and condemn false ones; and to teach revealed truths with unquestionable authority.[3] Although this vision was shared by many of the bishops and theologians who came to the Second Vatican Council (1962–1965), there were also many other bishops and theologians who were influenced by an existentialist vision that was emerging in European theological circles after World War II. From the existentialist perspective the Church and its teachings exist in and are influenced by changing cultures which challenge the Church to present the apostolic faith amidst ever new situations and thought forms that mark the unfolding of history. In the existentialist vision of the Church that we find at the Second Vatican Council the lived experience of faith holds the central place and theology's role is to find new ways to make the apostolic faith meaningful in contemporary Christian life and to evangelize those who have not yet heard the Gospel. This new perspective came from the renewal of biblical, historical, christological, ecclesiological and missiological studies in the twentieth century.

As John W. O'Malley, S.J. indicates, the presence of both of these views side by side in the documents of the Council and in subsequent Church documents has made it very difficult for the Church to move forward with a clear sense of ministry and mission:

> Distinctive of the *aggiornamento* of Vatican II in all its aspects was a keener awareness of cultural differences and the historical conditioning of all aspects of "the human side" of the face of the Church than any previous conciliar reform. This was the result of methodologies that many of the influential *periti* brought to the formulation of the documents of the Council, whether their specialty was liturgy, the Bible, Church history, ecumenics, Church-state relations, social problems or even systematic theology. The training of most of these men had caused them to modify or move away from the so-called Classicist mentality that had traditionally marked theological disciplines. The conflicts between these two mentalities underlies many of the documents of the Council and is still operative today in the debate over how to interpret them.[4]

In his own ministry and mission of service, Pope John Paul II tried to hold the essentialist and existentialist visions together out of his sense of responsibility to implement the documents of Vatican II as they are presented in their textual tension. His simultaneous beatification of the essentialist Pope Pius IX (1846–1878) and the existentialist Pope John XXIII (1958–1962) on September 3, 2000 is an excellent symbol of this commitment. However, *Ut Unum Sint* is also a symbol of the complexity of trying to hold the two visions together.

In the quotation above from *Ut Unum Sint*, Pope John Paul speaks of the Church being "taught by the events of history" and "committed to freeing herself from every purely human support in order to live in depth the Gospel law of the Beatitudes." He also says that the Church's "authority is exercised in the service of truth and charity." In responding to the call to be anew the People of God, we must be taught by the events of history and listen to what the Holy Spirit has said to Christian communities through their historical experience from the days of the Early Church to the present time. Understanding more clearly the unfolding historical experience of the People of God for two millenia and the *kenosis* involved in moving forward is the prelude to the reception of an ecclesial vision for the Pilgrim Church of the 21st century. This involves the challenge of a new appropriation of the Christian dichotomies that are held in truthful and creative tension by the Holy Spirit. For us to move forward we will require pastoral leadership that is exercised in the service of truth and charity.

As we reflect upon the meaning of a new appropriation of the Christian dichotomies that are held in truthful and creative tension by the Holy Spirit, we have the model of leadership exercised in the service of truth and charity in Pope John Paul's encyclical *Fides et Ratio*. In discussing the dichotomy of faith and reason, he emphasized the teaching of St. Thomas Aquinas that whatever its source, truth is of the Holy Spirit. It is wisdom, the highest of the gifts of the Holy Spirit, that enables us to hold together the truths we know from faith and the truths we know from reason in a single unified vision.[5] The Holy Spirit is at the very heart of the Church in its journey through history as the constant source of truth and charity, Who ever binds together in new ways all the dichotomies that are part of the Christian experience.

The Pope goes on to point out that philosophers understand that in order to maintain the unity of truth they need self-criticism, the correction of errors and the extension of the too-restricted terms in which they may have framed their thinking.[6] What the Pope says of philosophers is also true of theologians as they strive to formulate the faith of the Church in new historical and cultural situations. They need the gift of wisdom to understand the unity of truth which the Holy Spirit creates between Scripture, Tradition and the Magisterium as the Church moves through history and faces new challenges in articulating the Christian faith.

In discussing the dichotomy of faith and culture in *Fides et Ratio,* Pope John Paul said: "Lying deep in every culture, there appears this impulse toward a fulfillment. We may say, then, that culture itself has an intrinsic capacity to receive divine revelation."[7] Then cardinal, Joseph Ratzinger, in an address commenting on *Fides et Ratio* at St. Patrick's Seminary in Menlo Park, California on February 13, 1999 said: "Cultures are not fixed once and for all in a single form; they have the capacity to make progress and to be transformed as they also face the danger of decadence."[8] From the statements of both Pope John Paul and Cardinal Ratzinger we can see that all cultures have a capacity to receive divine revelation and that its reception can be transformative. Therefore there must be a modality by which a culture encounters divine revelation, and there must be a decision on the part of that culture to either receive or reject it.

Jesuit, Dominican, Franciscan and Augustinian missionaries became the modality for Japan to receive the proclamation of the Gospel in the 16th and 17th centuries. Although thousands of Japanese were initially converted to the Christian faith during the "Christian Century," for a variety of political, economical, social and religious reasons the Japanese people chose, ultimately, to reject Christianity in the first decades of the 17th century as inimical to their culture. They chose a policy of isolation from Western Christian influences until they were militarily forced to change their outlook by Western nations in the 19th century.

The complex historical situation of the sixteenth century in which the Japanese received the proclamation of the Gospel from European Roman Catholic missionaries did not eventuate in the people of Japan experiencing what then Cardinal Ratzinger said should be the truth of an encounter between faith and culture at its best: ". . . the proclamation of the Gospel in different cultures allows people to preserve their own cultural identity."[9] Both those who bring the Gospel from one cultural experience and those who receive it in another cultural experience are called to a process which involves a universalization of the faith transcending the particularity of each culture while offering a new inculturation which both respects the truths of the faith and the integrity of the culture receiving the faith.[10] For any culture to become a new historical expression of the sacramental mystery of the Church requires the work of the Holy Spirit, both in those who come to preach the Gospel and in those who hear and respond to the Gospel. What, then, might be an ecclesial and ministerial vision for servant leaders in the Post-Vatican II era?

AN ECCLESIAL VISION FOR THE PILGRIM CHURCH OF THE 21ST CENTURY

Chapter I of the Dogmatic Constitution on the Church, *Lumen Gentium,* presents the Church as a sacramental mystery with Christ, the Incarnate Word, at its center: "the Church, in Christ, is in the nature of sacrament—a sign and instrument, that is of communion with God and of unity among all men."[11] Jesus Christ is the sacrament of the encounter with God through the mystery of the Incarnation. The Church, as His body, is the extension of that sacramental mystery in the unfolding of God's great plan of salvation. As Cardinal Avery Dulles, S.J. has written: "The church as universal sacrament of salvation

culture in ways that maintain the apostolic faith while allowing it to come to a new and truthful expression of Christian life and thought. This often involves a profound *kenosis* on the part of those who preach and those who hear the message of the Gospel. Both must allow the Holy Spirit to bring them to a new hearing of the Gospel, which may involve letting go of the familiar to embrace a deepened experience of the Christian mystery in the journey of the Pilgrim Church.

The two thousand year pilgrimage of the People of God is marked by successful and unsuccessful attempts in cultural adaptation of the Gospel to new situations. The Fathers of the Second Vatican Council, in presenting their ecclesial vision for the Pilgrim Church of the 21st century in *Lumen Gentium,* were keenly aware of the constant need for renewal and reform if the Church is to be the sacrament of salvation for all people. What must servant leaders be and do to fulfill their ministry to the People of God in implementing the ecclesial vision of *Lumen Gentium* at the beginning of a new millennium?

THE MINISTRY AND MISSION OF SERVANT-LEADERS

This is precisely the question that the bishops gathered for the 10th Ordinary General Assembly of the Synod of Bishops in Rome from September 30-October 27, 2001 were asking themselves. After weeks of striving to listen together to what the Spirit is saying to local Churches throughout the world in which they exercise servant leadership, they produced their "Message to the People of God" entitled: "The Bishop: Weaver of Unity, Father and Brother of the Poor." They saw themselves called to be "servants of the Gospel of hope" in a broken and violent world that needs to hear anew the message of the Paschal Mystery. They sensed the seriousness of their mission: "In order to dialogue in truth with those who do not share our faith, our communion within the church must be simple and authentic so that all people, whatever their role within the church, 'preserve the unity of the Spirit through the bond of peace' (Eph. 4:3)."[19] In a world faced with monumental poverty in Asia, Africa and Latin America, the bishops sensed they had a special ministerial responsibility: "Just as we must struggle to free those oppressed by a poverty which is destructive, so there can be a kind of poverty which frees our energies for love and service. This is the Gospel poverty we want to practice."[20]

The bishops saw their ministry of service within local Churches as facilitating the many charisms that the Holy Spirit bestows on members of Christian communities: "As an expert weaver of unity, the bishop with his priests and deacons will discern and sustain all these charisms in their marvelous diversity."[21] Maintaining unity in diversity embraces not only the heart of the bishops' role in the life of the local Churches which they serve, but also the horizon for their role in promoting Christian unity: "Mindful of the irrevocable commitment of the Council to re-establish full communion among Christians, the bishop will lovingly commit himself to ecumenical dialogue and to developing the ecumenical understanding of his people."[22] The bishops saw their ministry as weavers of unity within the broader Christian community as uniting them to the vision of the Second Vatican Council that were so central to the ecumenical efforts of John Paul II: "With Pope John Paul II, we express our hope for a full return to that exchange of gifts which enriched the church of the first millennium" (*Novo Millennio Ineunte,* 48).[23]

The bishops' vision of the laity is also significant: "Today more than ever lay people are again playing their proper part in giving life to Christian communities, liturgical life, theological formation and charitable works."[24] From the bishops' perspective the involvement of lay men and women is crucial in bridging the gap between faith and culture through societal transformation in accord with the Gospel: "May they gather together in organized apostolates in the important struggle for justice and solidarity and so continue to bring hope and meaning to the world."[25] The bishops' are also conscious of the work of theologians in the dialogue of inculturation as the Church faces the rapidly changing world of the 21st century: "Developments in science and technology and the worldwide information revolution have forced us to examine the mystery of faith anew, with the energy, audacity and insight which characterized the fathers of the church, theologians, saints and pastors, who often did their work in times of trouble and change such as ours."[26] The bishops also recognize that the challenge of inculturation will involve all levels of their local Churches with theologians called to be weavers of unity just as they are: "But in order to explain the purity of the original Christian faith in a new and accessible language ever faithful to tradition, we need the particular contribution of skilled theologians."[27]

The vision of the bishop as servant leader that is presented in the "Message to the People of God" from the 2001 World Synod of Bishops is an important expression of the call for reform and renewal of the Church found in the seminal ecclesial vision of *Lumen Gentium.* This important plateau of understanding and praxis in ecclesiology that has been reached over the past forty years manifests some very important themes: 1) ecumenical dialogue in truth must flow from a communion within the Church that is simple and authentic; 2) struggling against poverty is an important Gospel witness; 3) discerning and maintaining in unity the diversity of the charisms present within local Churches is a significant dimension of the bishop's role; 4) the search for unity among separated Christians seeks a full return to the exchange of gifts that was present in the communion between the Churches of East and West during the first millennium; 5) the significant ministerial role of lay men and women is of immense importance for societal transformation; and 6) theologians need to provide a new and accessible language for the transmission of the faith that is both faithful to the apostolic tradition and reflective of the world-wide inculturation process that is underway. The progress that has been made since the close of the Second Vatican Council in developing a new vision of the mission and ministry of the Church has given us important directions for the future. However, to move to the next stage of reform and renewal, the Catholic Church must be willing to enter a new phase of *kenosis* . What kind of ecclesial *kenosis* is the Spirit calling the Churches of the 21st century to undergo so that they may be more fully the sacrament of the Christ the Servant, and what does that mean for the mission and ministry of servant leaders?

THE KENOSIS OF THE PILGRIM CHURCH OF THE 21ST CENTURY

The *kenosis* to which the Pilgrim Church is being called at this moment in its journey is letting go of certain historically conditioned facets of the Church's current self-understanding that are hindering the movement forward of the life and mission of the Church. Looking at the historical development of the ministry of leadership from Apostolic times to the present will help us to see the nature of some of the problems we are facing as we strive to move into the future. As we have seen earlier in this chapter, Pope John Paul II, in his encyclical *Ut Unum Sint,* said: "Taught by the events of history, the church is committed to freeing herself from every purely human support in order live in depth the Gospel law of the Beatitudes."[28] To be taught by history means that one must necessarily confront the tension between the essentialist and existentialist views that are present not only in the documents of the Second Vatican Council but also in subsequent Post-Conciliar documents. The essentialist vision often glosses over the complex historical processes that mark doctrinal and structural developments in the two thousand year history of Christianity. We can only engage in truthful dialogue within the Church and with our brothers and sisters of other religious traditions if we are willing to face the historical realities of the Church's history and accept the *kenosis* to which such an examination will ultimately call us.

In their historic "Common Declaration" of 1966, Pope Paul VI and the Archbishop of Canterbury, Michael Ramsey, set the stage for all subsequent ecumenical dialogue by calling for "a serious dialogue which, founded on the Gospels and on the ancient common traditions, may lead to that unity in truth, for which Christ prayed."[29] Both leaders sensed that Christian unity could only be achieved by a thoughtful re-appropriation of the shared vision of unity in diversity that marked the Eastern and the Western Churches of the first millennium, grounded in the New Testament, the Fathers of the Church and the seven mutually recognized Ecumenical Councils.

The Holy Spirit that guides the unfolding of the mystery of the life, death and resurrection of Christ, the sacrament of the encounter of humanity with God, is also the dynamic reality guiding the unfolding of the mystery of the Church in history as the sacrament of the crucified and risen Lord. The Church has always trusted the promise of its Lord as found in John 14:26: "The Advocate, the Holy Spirit that the Father will send in my name—He will teach you everything and remind you of all that I told you." The local churches of the New Testament are portrayed as communities that are enlivened and sustained by the work of the Holy Spirit through a variety of charisms which grace the members of the community in their diverse ministries of service. As the first Christian communities were inculturated in the Graeco-Roman world of the first century, the Holy Spirit provided the gifts necessary to guide the local communities, scattered in diverse parts of the Empire, in proclaiming the truths of the apostolic faith and establishing ministries that built up the life and work of its members. Because local churches, at times, faced different cultural challenges, the Spirit provided the gifts necessary to grace the experience of life in each Christian community. The history of the Church is the story of constant adaptation as the Church, guided by the Holy Spirit, strives to plant Christianity in new cultural circumstances while maintaining its fidelity to the Apostolic faith. The Second Vatican Council, in The Decree on the Church's Missionary Activity (*Ad gentes divinitus*), says:

> So too indeed, just as it happened in the economy of the incarnation, the young churches, which are rooted in Christ and built on the foundations of the apostles, take over all the riches of the nations which have been given to Christ as an inheritance (Ps. 2:8). They borrow from the customs, traditions, wisdom, teaching, arts and sciences of their people everything which could be used to praise the glory of the Creator, manifest the grace of the saviour, or contribute to the right ordering of Christian life.[30]

The perennial missionary activity of inculturation also requires the assistance of the Holy Spirit for the constant *kenosis* and wisdom that are necessary in the midst of adaptation to a new culture. The *kenosis* that is the letting go for missionaries involves a critical examination of their own cultural perspectives that allows them to put aside, when necessary, those things that might be hindrances to preaching the Gospel, while retaining those things that

The Church of the Christian empire in the fourth century left behind the house churches of the first three centuries and used the basilica, the Roman civic assembly hall, as the model for the new places of worship and ministry, now necessary to accommodate the vast numbers of converts from paganism entering the Christian faith. Constantine and his mother set the example by the basilicas they built for the Christian communities in Rome and Jerusalem. As the Roman Praetors presided over the law courts in the old Roman basilicas of the pagan Empire, the bishops of the Church now presided over public worship in the new Roman basilicas of the Christian Empire. In fact, the bishops, themselves, now held the powers of Praetors and could administer public justice when requested to do so. The positive side for the ministry of leadership as the Christian Church more fully inculturated itself into the Roman world was a clearly ordered threefold ministry of bishops, presbyters and deacons that provided instruction, liturgy and other ministerial services to local churches with the assistance of a number of auxiliary ministers who served their communities in various capacities. The negative side for the ministry of leadership that began with the Christian Empire was that the main task of bishops, presbyters and deacons was now maintaining the elaborate public liturgical life of the basilicas for communities of hundreds and sometimes thousands of people from whom they were increasingly separated both by their new clerical lifestyle and their participation in the civil power structures of the Empire. For the broader communities of baptized Christians in the Church of the basilicas there was the loss of the intimacy of community life and charismatic ministries they had known in the house churches. The universal call to ministry to the whole community of the baptized was replaced by the call to individual Christians to live virtuous lives as citizens of the Christian Empire.[33]

2. The Monastery as Minister

The Germanic invasions of the fourth and fifth centuries wrought havoc in much of the Western half of the Roman Empire. As the normal structures of civil government began to collapse under the strain of these incursions, the bishops often took the initiative in attempting to maintain some kind of order and in protecting their communities, insofar as possible, from the violence of the invaders. During the continuing breakup of the Western Roman Empire, symbolized in the founding of the Germanic kingdoms, it was the ministerial activity of the monasteries that would be the major factor in the inculturation of Christianity in the Early Medieval world between Gregory the Great (590–604) and Gregory VII (1073–1085). As the cities began to decline in many areas and the clergy of the local churches found themselves faced with the dual task of ministering to their own communities and trying to deal with either Arian Christian Germans such as the Visigoths or Pagan Germans such as the Franks, they were overwhelmed with the pastoral problems they were confronting.

The Celtic Church of Ireland, established by refugees from the continent and St Patrick from Roman Britain, was deeply monastic, missionary and devoted to study. Monks and nuns from Ireland initially, and later from Anglo-Saxon England, went to the Continent as missionaries to share with the Germanic tribes the Christian faith they had received. The monasteries they established became centers of evangelization and education through their schools and their preservation of the Classical and Christian literary heritage of the West. The liturgy that had been the primary ministerial function of bishops and presbyters and the care of the poor and sick that had at one time been the primary ministerial function of deacons in the urban centers of the Empire were now the ministerial focus of Abbots and their monks in the rural areas that predominated in Europe during the Early Middle Ages.

The positive side of the ministry of leadership provided by monk-missionaries of the great monastic centers in the Early Medieval world was their attempt to incarnate Christian teachings and values, such as justice and peace, in the minds and hearts of the Germanic peoples whom they were bringing into the Church. The negative side of the monastery as minister is that the life of the Abbot and his monks was now seen as the paradigm for all ministerial leadership, including the secular clergy. The vow of celibacy, the daily monastic office, monastic attire and a sense of detachment from worldly involvement, that were central to monasticism, were increasingly seen to be the ideal for diocesan clergy as well.[34] The gulf between the life experience of the People of God and their pastors was continuing to widen.

3. The Ministry as Hierarchy

The High Middle Ages with its rebirth of trade, towns and the beginning of the universities, where theologians developed ordered theological systems using the scholastic method, also saw the further development of trends in ministry that further widened the gulf between laity and clergy. Although literacy was increasing during this period, very few lay men and women in any congregation would have understood the Latin liturgy. The ministry of leadership was increasingly seen in terms of the power and authority received through the sacramental character given by the Holy Sprit in priestly ordination.[35] Unless they were kings or local lords, lay people had no voice in the selection of their pastors. During the High Middle Ages bishops and university-educated priests often held high posts in civil government and had little contact with

Baroque period of the Church, which extended for about two hundred years in its various phases from 1563 to 1760. The understanding of the ministry of leadership in this period centered on the careful organization of ministry around the papacy and the responsibility of those involved in pastoral care for the interior life of grace in those whom they served.[40] The priestly spirituality of the French school of Pierre Berulle, Charles de Condren and J.J. Olier saw the pastor or spiritual director as "a living extension of Christ in his sacrificial passion."[41] As Christ gave His life on the cross for the salvation of humankind, so the priest, through his ordination, shares in the mystery of Christ's passion and is called to be a mediator of grace to others through his ministry. The seminary education mandated by the Council of Trent was intended to train candidates for the priesthood in orthodox theology and to prepare them for a life of service by a program of formation that enabled them to become men of prayer, with the celebration of daily Mass, the recitation of the Divine Office and private meditation at the center of their lives. The spirituality of the Society of Jesus, founded by St. Ignatius Loyola, with its emphasis on a disciplined spiritual life, obedience to Church authorities and renewing the sacramental life of the laity, also played an important role in the vision of leadership held by the Church of the Baroque period. Just as the Post-Tridentine vision of ministry re-emphasized the hierarchical priesthood which the Reformers had denied, so, too, did it reaffirm the role of the papacy which the Reformers had also rejected. The new Protestant emphasis on the ministry of the pastor in the local congregation was countered by the Baroque vision of all ministries flowing from the ministry of the pope as the successor of St. Peter. The fourth vow of obedience to the Pope that was taken by the ministerial leaders of the Society of Jesus reflected the new view that the Papacy was the organizing principle of the Church.[42] The positive side of the Baroque understanding of ministry was that it affirmed that those engaged in pastoral care should be individuals committed to lives of holiness and service. The negative side of the Post-Tridentine vision of the Church and ministry was that a network of local Churches under their bishops with their own geographical and cultural identity was now seen as dangerous.[43] The concept of unity in diversity that had been the strength and hallmark of the Church in the East and in the West during the first millennium of the Christian era was replaced by the idea that true unity could only be found in a uniformity of faith and practice that was under the constant oversight of the Bishop of Rome.

6. The Romanticization of Ministry

Although the 18th century Enlightenment, the French Revolution and the Napoleonic era took their toll on the Church, early 19th century Romanticism, with its accompanying Catholic renewal, joined interest in mysticism and the presence of God in the world, ritual and religious life to a revived Baroque Catholic vision.[44] Many new religious communities, engaged in a variety of educational, social services and missionary ministries, were established in the 19th century. While adopting the major features that marked the Baroque vision of ministry, they also placed a new emphasis on devotions to Christ, Mary and the saints, that was manifest in the development of personal piety with a strong emotional content.

As the 19th century world seemed to become more secular and hostile, the Church began to turn inward and to become a world unto itself. The Church became, in many instances, a kind of haven where one could find peace in the grandeur of the past, manifest in Neo-Gothic cathedrals and churches filled with stained glass showing the lives of Christ, Mary and the saints. Pilgrimage shrines became places one could visit to find interior solace in the midst of a world that often seemed increasingly anti-Catholic. The ministry of leadership sought, through the sacraments, especially penance and the Eucharist, to keep the life of grace alive in individuals by encouraging them to personal holiness and the exercise of Christian values in a secular world. St. John Vianney (1786–1859), the Cure of the small French village of Ars, who often spent as many as eighteen hours a day hearing confessions and offering counsel, became the model for a true pastor totally concerned about the spiritual welfare of his own parishoners and others who sought his help in trying to live authentic Christian lives in the midst of a secular society.

Missionaries, who sought to bring Christianity to the peoples of Africa, Asia and Oceania, were also an important dimension of the Church. Their missionary efforts were motivated by a deep desire to bring the Gospel to the whole world, but the missionaries seemed, at times, to equate Christianization with Europeanization. The kind of *kenosis* that a true inculturation would have required often did not happen, and Christianity, in many cases, came to be seen as a foreign way of life that did not respect the traditional values of the culture. The ferocity of the violence against Christian missionaries in 1900 during the Boxer Revolution in China was indicative of the level of fear that was present in many native leaders who came to identify Christianity with Europeanization and the undermining of the values that were at the heart of Chinese culture.

By 1950 the ecclesial Romanticism of the 19th century was coming to an end. New ways of thinking were emerging as a result of important biblical, patristic, historical, liturgical, ecumenical and missiological research that would provide a new theological vision of the Church and its ministry for the Second Vatican Council. The positive side of the vision of the Church and ministry that Romanticism provided was a sense of security and confidence given by the traditional teachings and worship patterns of the Church amidst a secular world that seemed ever more hostile to the values of Christianity. The negative side of the Romantic vision was that it tended to isolate the Church and its ministers from the mainstream of modern life and thought, thus removing the Church from exercising a significant role in the development of societal values in a world deeply in need of a meaningful vision of Christian life.

What does the history of the Church and its ministry of leadership in each of the six periods that we have discussed tell us concretely about the kind of *kenosis* to which the Holy Spirit is calling the Pilgrim Church of the 21st century? By linking one of the themes of the "Message to the People of God" from the 2001 World Synod of Bishops to each of the six periods of history that we have discussed, we can come to a better understanding of the various dimensions of the next stage of *kenosis* to which the People of God and their servant leaders are being called. Firstly, the bishops said that ecumenical dialogue must flow from a communion within the Church that is simple and authentic. Early Christianity, that began as a small religious movement with its members scattered throughout the Roman world, eventually became the official religion of the Empire. The changes in self-understanding which that transformation evoked in Christian communities and their leaders, as they responded to incredible new challenges of inculturating the Gospel in the Roman world, were profound. The Church became structurally more complex and assumed a role in public life that placed the leaders of the Church in positions of power that involved a new understanding of their responsibilities and their authority. Since bishops were now not only spiritual leaders, but also public officials of the Empire, the possibility of their losing sight of their pastoral mission and becoming absorbed in the power and political struggles involved in holding public office was very real. In order that communion within the Church be truly simple and authentic, as the Synod of Bishops proposed, there must be a constant *kenosis* on the part of those in pastoral leadership that lets go of anything in their ministry that bespeaks the exercise of power rather than service. The lives and ministries of Church leaders must bespeak simplicity and authenticity both to those whom they serve as pastors and to the communities where they live if they are to be servant leaders for the Pilgrim Church of the 21st century.

Secondly, the Synod Bishops said that the Gospel poverty they wanted to practice was "struggling to free those oppressed by a poverty which is destructive, so there can be a kind of poverty which frees our energies for love and service."[45] The great monasteries of the Early Middle Ages in their foundation period were centers of ministry for the people of the area, and the monks were initially deeply concerned about caring for the poor and living poorly themselves. However, as time went by and they began to receive numerous benefactions in the form of property and goods, their lifestyle began to change. Abbots and their monks became more like the local lords involved in the oversight and care of their vast estates. Monks involved in the administration of great monastic estates began to have less direct involvement with the poor, and great abbeys, such as Cluny, built magnificent monastic buildings filled with art treasures that did not reflect the poverty of spirit that frees people's energies for love and service. The service of the poor and the poverty of spirit that the Synod of Bishops proposed for servant leaders requires a *kenosis* that enables bishops and pastors to be sufficiently freed from administrative tasks so that they have freedom to be among the people whom they are called to serve, especially the poor. There must also be a *kenosis* of lifestyle that eliminates bishops or pastors living in residences or having possessions that are indicative of wealth and power, but are inappropriate for those called to minister to the Pilgrim People of God in the 21st century. The pattern of Christ the poor man, who came to be the servant of the poor, must be the pattern of life for servant leaders if they are to be true witnesses of the meaning of the Gospel they proclaim.

Thirdly, the Synod of Bishops said that "As an expert weaver of unity, the bishop with his priest and deacons will discern and sustain all these charisms [of the local Church] in their marvelous diversity." The hierarchical pattern that the Church of the High Middle Ages took from Pseudo-Dionysius saw the clergy as the active agents in ministry and the laity as passive and obedient recipients of clerical ministry and authority. The full realization of the return to the New Testament pattern of ministry with local church communities that are enlivened and sustained by the work of the Holy Spirit through a variety of charisms requires further *kenosis* on the part of servant-leaders. We must move away from the hierarchical understanding of the Church that emerged in the High Middle Ages and adopt the vision of circles of ministry described by Thomas O'Meara, O.P.:

> The communal leader stands not over against or in competition with other ministries, but as a leader who enables . . . The model of concentric circles helps here: it stands in contrast to the line dividing this group from that, a division unable to recognize degrees of ministry . . . Here all ministries are based upon the under- lying animating force of the Spirit in the community and unfold from charism and personality vitalized by baptism and drawn to ministry. Circles of ministry indicate a similarity in ministry but also point to differences and distinctions among degrees of ministry ranging from leadership to occasional services. The distinctions and differences are initiated by baptism, commissioning and ordination but are ultimately based upon the goal of the ministry.[46]

Letting go of the hierarchical model of the Middle Ages and embracing the model of circles of ministry would enable servant leaders to become the weavers of unity sustaining all the charisms of the local Church in their marvelous diversity that the Synod of Bishops envisioned.

Fourthly, the Synod of Bishops, quoting Pope John Paul's understanding of the search for Christian unity, said that they were committed to a "full return to that exchange of gifts which enriched the church of the first millenium."[47] The Reformers' vision of the Church included a return to the unity in diversity that characterized the first millennium rather than the unity that became uniformity under papal centralization in the 16th century. The Protestant emphasis upon the autonomy of the local congregation or the regional Church, and the rejection of a universal Church that seemed intrusive and lacking in true Gospel values, must be taken seriously in current ecumenical dialogues. While the documents of the Second Vatican Council emphasized the universal Church as a communion of local churches united under the leadership of the Bishop of Rome, the years following the Council have not yet witnessed the kind of lawful autonomy of local Churches witnessing to unity in diversity that will be necessary for the accomplishment of Christian unity. Neither the Orthodox Churches of the East, nor the Protestant Churches of the West will accept a kind of Christian unity that does not allow for the diversity of expression in theology, liturgy, ministry and spirituality that characterized the first millennium. For a full return to the exchange of gifts that was present in the communion between the Churches of East and West during the first millennium, servant leaders of the Roman Catholic Church must engage in a *kenosis* of decentralization that moves away from centralized uniformity and returns to local Churches the freedom and diversity that is rightfully theirs. For there to be Christian unity in the Pilgrim Church of the 21st century the People of God in local churches, in collaboration with their pastors, must call upon Rome to return to them the freedom in decision-making in matters such as choice of leadership, liturgy, and ministry, which expresses the unity in diversity that is their right and heritage from the Apostolic Church.

Fifthly, the Synod of Bishops said that "Today more than ever lay people are again playing their proper part in giving to Christian communities, liturgical life, theological formation and charitable works."[48] The Church of the Counter-Reformation saw true ministry as centered in the work of celibate clergy, while religious sisters and brothers and some laity engaged in apostolates that were helpful in assisting the clergy to meet the ministerial needs of the Church. The letter of the Bishops rightfully recognizes the crucial and proper role that lay men and women are increasingly playing as full-time or part-time ministers in local Churches. However, as we face the future, we need to realize that our current understanding of ministry requires that we undergo further *kenosis* both for the sake of meeting the future ministerial needs of the Roman Catholic Church, and to move toward full Christian unity.

Listening to what the Holy Spirit is saying to the churches at any point in the journey of the People of God means taking seriously both the history of the Church and our own experience. The current discipline of celibacy for priests in the Roman Catholic Church corresponds neither to the discipline of the Eastern Churches nor to the Protestant Churches. Priests of Eastern Rite Churches in union with Rome are allowed to marry, and Protestant ministers who have become Roman Catholics and wished to continue their ministry have been allowed to live as married priests. Canon 247:1 speaks of celibacy as "a special gift of God,"[49] and the Eastern Churches from Apostolic times have also recognized that priesthood and celibacy are different gifts. A number of Protestant Churches, including Anglicans and Lutherans, with whom Catholics are in serious dialogue about the unity of the Church, have chosen to ordain women. Servant leaders within the Roman Church must continue to listen to the experience of our sister Churches as well as the experience of the People of God in the Roman Catholic Church and be willing to embrace a *kenosis* in our current understanding of the ministry that would allow married men as well as women to be ordained to the priesthood. For the Pilgrim Church of the 21st century to come to the fullness of life and service to which it is called, servant leaders must be willing to listen more carefully to the experiential wisdom of the People of God and other Christian Churches if we are to fulfill our mission from the Risen Lord to be the sacrament of salvation to the whole world.

Sixthly, the Synod of Bishops said: "in order to explain the purity of the original Christian faith in a new and accessible language ever faithful to tradition, we need the particular contribution of skilled theologians."[50] The Romantic vision of the Church in the 19th century tended to be fearful of new ideas and the developments that were taking place in biblical, historical and theological scholarship. But the Bishops recognized that we need a new and accessible language in which to proclaim the Christian faith. Theologians are being asked to contribute to this work of a new evangelization that will require awareness of the complexities of the variety of cultural experiences in which the faith must be proclaimed in the 21st century. The *kenosis* that will be asked of servant leaders in this process will be to let go of old formulations of the faith that no longer convey the Christian faith in clear and accessible language. In their work of formulating the Apostolic faith anew, theologians need to listen carefully not only to scripture, tradition, the teaching of the Church across the centuries, pronouncements of the magisterium and current scholarship in relevant fields, but also to the experience of the People of God. If we do not listen to the voice of the Spirit speaking through the People of

40. O' Meara, *Theology of Ministry*, 117.

41. O'Meara, *Theology of Ministry*, 117.

42. O'Meara, *Theology of Ministry*, 118.

43. O'Meara, *Theology of Ministry*, 118.

44. O'Meara, *Theology of Ministry*, 124.

45. Synod of Bishops, "The Bishop," *Origins* 31: 22: 368.

46. O'Meara, *Theology of Ministry*, 157–158.

47. Synod of Bishops, "The Bishop," *Origins* 31: 22: 369.

48. Synod of Bishops, "The Bishop," *Origins* 31: 22: 369.

49. The Canon Law Society of America, *Code of Canon Law: Latin-English Edition,* (Washington D.C.: Canon Law Society of America, 1983), 85.

50. Synod of Bishops, "The Bishop," *Origins* 31: 22: 370.

Chapter Five

The Bishop of Rome as the Servant of the Servants of God unto Unity in Diversity

INTRODUCTION

In his encyclical letter, *Ut Unum Sint,* Pope John Paul II writes: "The bishop of Rome must fervently make his own Christ's prayer for that conversion which is indispensable for 'Peter' to be able to serve his brethren. I earnestly invite the faithful of the Catholic Church and all Christians to share in this prayer. May all join me in praying for this conversion."[1]

Pope John Paul II profoundly realized that for the Church to fulfill its mission of service in proclaiming the Gospel to the men and women of the 21st century all Christians need to see in the Petrine ministry the pattern of discipleship that exemplifies witness of the Resurrection. He also knew that he had a special responsibility to offer the example of the path of conversion that must be followed by all servant leaders, and hence he rightly asked for the prayers of all Christians.

Besides asking for prayerful assistance in understanding how to exercise his ministry for the sake of Christian unity, the Pope made a further request: "I insistently pray to the Holy Spirit to shine His light upon us, enlightening all the pastors and theologians of our churches, that we may seek—together of course—the forms in which this ministry may accomplish a service of love recognized by all concerned."[2] Pope John Paul II realized, as do we who are pastors and theologians, the depth of the challenge that has been set before us as we strive to fulfill with integrity our co-responsibility with him to seek the unity of the Church:

> This is an immense task, which we cannot refuse and which I cannot carry out by myself. Could not the real but imperfect communion existing between us persuade church leaders and their theologians to engage with me in a patient and

fraternal dialogue on this subject, a dialogue in which, leaving useless contro-
versies behind, we could listen to one another, keeping before us only the will
of Christ for his church and allowing ourselves to be deeply moved by his plea
'that they may all be one. . .so that the world may believe that you have sent me'
(John 17:21)?[3]

As we respond to Pope John Paul's invitation to dialogue about the Papacy,
we want to express the theological perspective that we are using in this book
to enter into the conversation that the Pope has requested. We believe that the
truths of the Christian faith are neither absolute nor relative in their expression. Rather they are pneumatic, that is to say they are formed and guided by
the Holy Spirit in their meaning and interpretation: "The Holy Spirit that the
Father will send in my name will teach you everything and remind you of all
that I told you."(John 14:26). The Spirit guides the Church in interpreting
scriptural texts and tradition in terms of the needs of the People of God at that
time as they attempt to live in each era in accord with the Apostolic faith. But
every scriptural text, in order to be correctly interpreted, must constantly be
seen in relationship to the scriptures as a whole which serve as a pneumatic
guide to authentic interpretation and a pneumatic corrective to misinterpretation. The failure to interpret any New Testament text without seeing it in relationship to the whole of the New Testament at any point in the history of the
Church will require a pneumatic corrective at a future point. This pneumatic
corrective is present when the Holy Spirit calls, through prophetic voices, for
a re-interpretation of a text or texts that more fully corresponds to the truth of
the Apostolic faith. The Holy Spirit uses the prophetic voices of theologians
and the *consensus fidelium* to bring about necessary correctives as the Pilgrim
Church seeks to preach the Gospel in a new stage of its journey through history. In this Chapter we will look at the New Testament's presentation of the
ministry of St. Peter and the subsequent development of the Petrine office
throughout the history of the Church to see what pneumatic correctives may
be necessary if we are to hear what the Holy Spirit is saying to the Churches
at the beginning of the 21st century.

PETER: DISCIPLE, APOSTLE AND MARTYR

In discussing the Petrine office, we need to keep in mind a dimension of the
apostolic tradition that is present in the New Testament and is of profound importance for the early Church: the constant linking of Peter and Paul as the
prime apostolic witnesses of the Church of Rome. Pope John Paul wrote in
Ut Unum Sint:

The bishop of Rome is the bishop of the church which preserves the mark of the martyrdom of Peter and of Paul: "By a mysterious design of providence it is at Rome that [Peter] concludes his journey in following Jesus, and it is at Rome that he gives his greatest proof of love and fidelity. Likewise Paul, the apostle of the gentiles, gives his supreme witness at Rome. In this way the church of Rome became the church of Peter and Paul.[4]

The whole of the New Testament is the providential gift of the Risen Christ to his Church. The Holy Spirit serves each generation, guiding its interpretation of the word of God and providing the pneumatic guide to authentic interpretation and the pneumatic corrective to misinterpretation of any dimension of the apostolic faith. Together the Petrine ministry and the Pauline ministry witness to this truth.

In looking at the roles of Peter and Paul in the New Testament, we shall use Oscar Cullman's very significant work, *Peter: Disciple, Apostle, Martyr*, to present an understanding of their apostolic ministries that seems to have the best grounding in historical and exegetical evidence and research. There are a number of important questions that we need to consider as we engage in ecumenical dialogues searching for Christian unity. What is the nature of authority that is given by Christ to Peter in Matthew 16? How is it different from the authority that is given to all the apostles in Matthew 18, and later on to Paul in his call to apostleship by the Risen Lord on the road to Damascus? What is the nature of the authority that is passed on to the successors of the apostles in general, and to the bishop of Rome in particular? Is the authority of the bishop of Rome unique, or is it the preeminent symbol of what is given to all the bishops as successors of the apostles?

In exploring the mystery of Peter, Cullman begins with Peter the disciple. He writes:

> Among the disciples of Jesus, Peter, according to the united witness of the gospel tradition, occupies a peculiarly representative position. This does not mean, however, that during the lifetime of Jesus he possessed the role of *leader* in relation to his fellow-disciples. He is rather at all times their *spokesman*, their representative in good as in bad action. But he gives them no commissions in the name of Jesus and the Master nowhere entrusts to him such a function for the period of his earthly life. The three passages, Matthew 16:16 ff., Luke 22:31f. and John 21:15ff. in which he is charged with a special obligation towards his brothers, all refer to the future, to the time after the death of Jesus. Thus the gospel tradition knew how to distinguish between the position of Peter before and after the death of Jesus.[5]

The clarity of the Gospels in expressing the representative role of Peter as disciple is important because we see him in the full range of his humanity. In

Matthew 16:16–19, after confessing that Jesus is the Messiah and being given the role of "Rock" in the foundation of the Church, Peter then tries to deter Jesus from going to Jerusalem to suffer and die. He is told, in Matthew 16:23: "Get behind me, Satan! You are an obstacle to me. You are thinking not as God does, but as human beings do." Peter and the other disciples are not only capable of understanding the mission of Jesus and their role in it with the help of God's assistance, but they are also capable of misunderstanding both because of their own frailty and limitations. The two texts side by side give us an example of one New Testament text functioning as a pneumatic corrective for a possible misinterpretation of another New Testament text.

As Cullman indicates, understanding the full mystery of Peter's discipleship with both his strengths and his weaknesses, as presented in the Gospels, helps us to appreciate more fully the meaning of Peter the Apostle as we meet him in the Acts of the Apostles:

> For the period following the death of Jesus the question concerning the unique position of Peter presents itself in another way. The disciple becomes the apostle of the crucified and risen Lord . . . According to the sources at our disposal, the death and resurrection of Jesus creates for Peter a completely changed situation. This is true in two respects. In the first place, from this time on his unique role appears no longer merely as that of a representative; in view of the physical absence of the Lord, it naturally appears in the leadership of the small community of disciples.[6]

The first twelve chapters of Acts, which present the life of the early Christian communities, describe the ministry of leadership exercised by Peter as the head of the apostolic Church with its headquarters in Jerusalem. Chapters thirteen through twenty-eight of Acts detail the ministry of leadership of Paul in his missionary journeys, his establishing local churches in the cities of the Empire and, finally, his arrival in Rome as a prisoner to plead his innocence before the Emperor of the charges made against him by the Jewish authorities in Jerusalem.

The trajectories of the apostolic ministries of Peter and Paul, as they unfold in Acts, and the interaction of the two apostles, both in Acts and other books of the New Testament, offer us an important perspective for the early Church's understanding of the Petrine ministry and the Pauline ministry. We need to pay attention both to what is said and what is not said about the ministries of the two apostles. In chapters one through twelve of Acts, Peter is the servant leader who speaks in the name of the apostolic community. Yet Peter always ministers in communion with the other apostles. He leads by serving their common mission to preach the Gospel, heal the sick, care for the poor and live as a community formed by the experience of new life that flows from the redemptive work of the crucified and risen Lord and is sustained by the gift of the Holy Spirit. In accord with Jesus' teaching in Luke 22:26, Peter seeks to serve, and not to rule, and now strengthens his brother apostles in their common ministry through the prayer of Christ, as promised in Luke 22: 32. After his miraculous release from prison during Herod's persecution, as recorded in Acts 12, Peter yields his servant leadership of the Jerusalem Church to James the brother of the Lord and becomes the leader of the mission to the scattered Jewish Christian communities of the Empire. Cullmann succinctly summarizes the Petrine ministry described in the first twelve chapters of Acts:

> The Apostle Peter, in the first period after the death of Jesus, leads the Primitive Church in Jerusalem; he then leaves Jerusalem, where the leadership passes over to James; and from then on, by commission of the Primitive Church and in dependence on it, he stands at the head of the Jewish Christian mission.[7]

Although Paul was originally a persecutor of the nascent Christian Church, he became an apostle with Peter and the eleven through his encounter with the Risen Christ in his conversion experience. He believed that he had received the same apostolic authority of servant leadership as had the other apostles and that he and Peter shared a parallel responsibility for the proclamation of the Gospel. Speaking of his first encounter with Peter after his conversion, he writes: "Then after three years I went up to Jerusalem to confer with Kephas and remained with him for fifteen days. But I did not see any other of the apostles, only James the brother of the Lord" (Gal. 1:18–19). Paul recognized the significant role of the servant leadership of Peter within the apostolic college as well as the role of James the brother of the Lord who succeeded him as head of the Jerusalem Church. Paul also acknowledged the leadership of Peter and James fourteen years later at the gathering of the Council of Jerusalem:

> Then after fourteen years I again went up to Jerusalem with Barnabas, taking Titus along also. I went up in accord with a revelation, and I presented to them the gospel that I preach to the Gentiles—but privately to those of repute—so that I might not be running, or have run, in vain . . . But from those who were reputed to be important (what they once were makes no difference to me; God shows no partiality)—those of repute made me add nothing. On the contrary, when they saw that I had been entrusted with the gospel to the uncircumcised, just as Peter to the circumcised, for the one who worked in Peter for an apostolate to the circumcised worked also in me for the Gentiles, and when they recognized the grace bestowed upon me, James and Kephas and John, who were reputed to be pillars, gave me and Barnabas their right hands in partnership, that we should go the Gentiles and they to the circumcised. Only, that we were to be mindful of the poor, which is the very things I was eager to do (Gal. 2:1–2; 7–10).

After the Council of Jerusalem Paul felt it was necessary to offer Peter a pneumatic corrective at Antioch when the latter was not acting in accord with the evangelical understanding that had been reached by the apostolic community:

> And when Kephas came to Antioch, I opposed him to his face because he was clearly wrong. For, until some people came from James, he used to eat with the Gentiles; but when they came, he began to draw back and separate himself, because he was afraid of the circumcised. And the rest of the Jews also acted hypocritically along with him, with the result that even Barnabas was carried away by their hypocrisy. But when I saw that they were not on the right road in line with the truth of the gospel, I said to Kephas in front of all, "If you, though a Jew, are living like a Gentile and not like a Jew, how can you compel the Gentiles to live like Jews?" (Gal. 2:11–14).

The encounter between Peter and Paul at Antioch is the New Testament witness that the Petrine ministry and the Pauline ministry are complementary dimensions of maintaining the apostolic faith. The Pauline ministry sustains the exercise of the Petrine ministry as a continuance of apostolic witness in accord with the truth of the gospel. The Holy Spirit is always guiding the community as a whole, and when a leader within the community moves away from the truth of the gospel, the Holy Spirit provides a pneumatic corrective through another leader.

The New Testament contains no direct reference to Peter's ministry in Rome, but we do know of Paul's presence in the Eternal City through the final chapter of the Acts of the Apostles. Although there is uncertainty about the authorship and date of the two New Testament letters, I and II Peter, they both open with a greeting in Peter's name and are thus valuable as we try to understand the ministries and relationship of the two apostles. We read in I Peter 5:1–5:

> So I exhort the presbyters among you, as a fellow presbyter and witness to the sufferings of Christ and one who has a share in the glory to be revealed. Tend the flock of God in your midst, [overseeing] not by constraint but willingly, as God would have it, not for shameful profit but eagerly. Do not lord it over those assigned to you, but be examples to the flock. And when the chief shepherd is revealed, you will receive the unfading crown of glory. Likewise, you younger members, be subject to the presbyters.

And in II Peter: 3:15–16 we read:

> And consider the patience of our Lord as salvation, as our beloved brother Paul, according to the wisdom given to him, also wrote to you, speaking of these

things as he does in all his letters. In them there are some things hard to understand that the ignorant and unstable distort to their own destruction, just as they do the other scriptures.

The author of II Peter wanted to affirm the harmony between Peter and Paul, who is cited for his wisdom, while also indicating the complexity of Paul's writings and the possibility of their being distorted. The author of I Peter has Peter as a presbyter exhorting fellow presbyters to be worthy shepherds in the pattern of Christ. The shepherd image certainly resonates with the portrayal of Peter in John 21 as the one to whom Jesus entrusts the care of the flock and as the shepherd who lays down his life in the pattern of the Lord:

> Amen, amen, I say to you, when you were younger, you used to dress yourself and go where you wanted; but when you grow old, you will stretch out your hands, and someone else will dress you and lead you where you do not want to go. He said this signifying by what kind of death he would glorify God. And when he had said this, he said to him, "Follow me" (John 21:18–19).

Peter the disciple and apostle is finally to become Peter the martyr.

Cullmann summarizes his historical discussion of Peter: disciple, apostle, martyr with the following remarks:

> We must say that during the lifetime of Peter, he held a pre-eminent position among the disciples; that after Christ's death he presided over the church at Jerusalem in the first years; that he then became the leader of the Jewish Christian mission; that in this capacity, at a time which cannot be more closely determined but probably occurred at the end of his life, he came to Rome and there, after very short work, died as a martyr under Nero.[8]

When Paul wrote his Letter to the Romans in the late 50's C.E., there was religious tension not only between Jews and Jewish Christians, but also between Jewish Christians and Gentile Christians of the capital city. The Christian house churches there must also have represented the same kind of ethnic diversity from all over the Empire that we see reflected in Chapter 2 of the Acts of Apostles. The vision of salvation for both Jews and Gentiles through the death and resurrection of Jesus Christ that Paul presents in his letter is a masterful attempt to bring harmony and peace to a complex church, which he neither founded nor has yet visited. We know from Paul's Letter to the Galatians that he and Peter had already faced a similar conflictual situation together between Jewish Christians and Gentile Christians in Antioch. Paul finally came to Rome as a prisoner around 61 C.E. and, according to Acts, was under house arrest there for two years. He seems subsequently to have left the Eternal City for some period of time perhaps going west to Spain or back to the East. According to Eusebius he later returned to Rome and died as a martyr: "There is evidence that, having been brought to trial, the apostle set out on the ministry of preaching, and having appeared a second time in the same city found fulfillment in martyrdom."[9] Outside of the cryptic reference to Babylon at the end of I Peter, there is no other New Testament text that explicitly refers to Peter's ministry in Rome or to his death there. The earliest reference that we have from the post-apostolic period of the death of both Peter and Paul at Rome is from the letter sent by Clement of Rome to the Church at Corinth around 96 C.E.:

> It was due to jealousy and envy that the greatest and most holy pillars were persecuted and fought to the death. Let us pass in review the good Apostles: Peter, who through unmerited jealousy underwent not one or two, but many hardships and after thus giving testimony, departed for the place of glory that was his due. Through jealousy and strife Paul demonstrated how to win the prize of patient endurance . . .when he had given testimony before the authorities, ended his earthly career and was taken up into the holy place as the greatest model of endurance.[10]

Clement speaks of jealousy and strife that led to the death of Peter and Paul. Since Clement is using this example in trying to restore order within the Christian community at Corinth, it could well be that Peter and Paul had come to Rome to try to restore unity within the complex reality of the diverse Christian communities gathered in the house churches of the city and that they were ultimately victims of a broader tragedy of persecution under Nero. Cullman observes:

> When Clement, in this very passage, writes that Peter had to suffer "on account of unrighteous jealousy," and Paul "on account of jealousy and strife," . . .this in the context of our letter can only mean that they were victims of jealousy from persons who counted themselves members of the Christian Church. In saying this we naturally do not mean that they were martyred or perhaps murdered by other Christians, but that the magistrates were encouraged by the attitude of some members of the Christian Church, and perhaps by the fact that they turned informers, to take action against others.[11]

The apostles Peter and Paul come together at the end of their lives under the pneumatic guidance of the Holy Spirit not to rule the Church of Rome, but to lay down their lives in martyrdom for the unity of the Christian community, as the ultimate expression of the meaning of servant leadership.

What then can we learn from the New Testament presentation of the apostolic ministry of Peter and Paul that can be helpful to us we try to understand the ministry of the Bishop of Rome as the servant of the servants of God unto unity in the Church of the 21st century? It seems to us that we can now try to respond to three important questions that we posed earlier in this chapter. First, what is the nature of the authority that is given by Christ to Peter in Matthew 16? Cullman says:

> Jesus promises Peter that he will build upon him the earthly people of God; he promises that in this people Peter will have the leadership, both in missionary work and in organization. His immediate thought, just as in John 21:16ff., probably deals only with the time of Peter. But even if he explicitly had in view the period following Peter's death as the time of the building of the Church, what is said of Peter as the Rock refers only to him, the historical apostle; he represents once for all the earthly foundation, the beginning who supports the whole structure of the *ekklesia* that is to be built in the future.[12]

This is not to say that the bishop of Rome is not meant to share in the ministry of oversight of the Church that is assigned to Peter and the other apostles, but is meant to say that the ministry of Peter as the foundation stone is unique for the Church of all times and places and cannot be passed on to anyone else.

Second, how is the authority that is given to Peter different from that given to the other apostles, including Paul? Cullmann says:

> The leadership of the Church by Peter is also *apostolic leadership*, and so belongs to the never to be repeated Rock role, the laying of the foundation . . .But on the other hand, we have pointed out many times that in contrast to the office of the apostle, that of the leader in the Church continues. Thus we here must pay attention to two things; one the one hand, to the non-transferable character of the leadership of the Primitive Church by Peter; on the other hand, to the fact that there must also be leadership later in the Church.[13]

Peter stands as the head of the apostolic college, which includes Paul. He is their visible leader and the sign of their unity in Christ. Paul is seen to exercise a corrective function within the apostolic college, when he calls Peter, at Antioch, to fulfill his apostolic ministry in line with the truth of the Gospel. Guided by the Holy Spirit the Pauline ministry serves as a pneumatic corrective when the Petrine ministry fails to be the pneumatic guide for Gospel living that it is meant to be for the Christian community.

Third, what is the nature of the authority that is passed on to the successors of the apostles in general and to the bishop of Rome in particular? Cullmann writes:

> Thus it is absolutely irreconcilable with the New Testament concept of apostleship when a saying on the founding of the Church that was addressed to an apostle is

simply referred to future bishops. Elders and bishops certainly do take the place of
the apostles, and one may call them successors, even if this expression opens the
way to misunderstandings. But in any case it must not be forgotten for a moment
that they occupy a completely different position, and they must not be regarded as
successors in the sense of "continuers of the apostolic function." They are successors in the chronological sense, but not in their nature. *Their function follows that
of the apostles, but as a fundamentally different one* . . . The apostles give over to
those men the leadership, *but not their own apostolic office*. For they knew well that
they could not hand this on at all since it could only be given by Jesus himself directly and *without mediation* (Gal 1:12ff1). Therefore they did not install any
"apostles" as successors in leadership, but rather "bishops" and "elders."[14]

There are, indeed, successors to the apostles who share, in a limited way, their
apostolic authority, but we must be very careful to distinguish clearly the limits of that authority in accord with the New Testament so that it reflects the
truthfulness of their role as bishops and elders and not as apostles, since the
latter office is unique to those chosen by Jesus himself and cannot be handed
on. With regard to Peter and the Church at Rome, Cullman writes:

> Of certain *individual churches* we can say that by instituting local church heads
> the apostles, in their unique capacity as apostles, thus created the first bishops
> of these churches. This, to be sure, says nothing at all as to who after them is to
> choose subsequent bishops. The apostle Peter, on the other hand, never estab-
> lished a bishop as the leader of the *entire Church*, and above all he himself never
> gave distinction to any Church *except Jerusalem* as the seat of his own leader-
> ship of the entire Church. *For even if, after his leadership of the Jerusalem
> church, he temporarily as apostolic missionary was the leader of still other
> churches, yet so much at least is definite, that when he was there he was only the
> leader of those single churches, and in no case leader of the entire Church. Pe-
> ter was the leader of the entire Church only at Jerusalem.* Concerning Antioch,
> indeed, . . . there is a tradition, first appearing in the course of the second cen-
> tury, according to which Peter was its bishop. The assertion that he was Bishop
> of Rome we first find at a much later time. From the second half of the second
> century we do possess texts that mention the apostolic *foundation* of Rome, and
> at this time, which is indeed rather late, this foundation is traced back to *Peter
> and Paul*, an assertion that cannot be supported historically. Even here, however,
> nothing is said as yet of an episcopal office of Peter. But even if Peter did oc-
> cupy in Rome an episcopal position, this could hold good at the most for the *lo-
> cal* church in Rome, for it is a fixed fact that *at that time*, in the sixth decade of
> the first century, Rome still played no leading role in the Church at large, and
> Peter did not rule the entire Church from Rome.[15]

From an historical and New Testament perspective, we cannot say with certi-
tude that Peter was ever Bishop of Rome or that he ruled the entire Church

from Rome. However, what we can affirm clearly is the ecumenical perspective presented in the ARCIC 1982 Statement on "Authority in the Church II:"

> The New Testament contains no explicit record of a transmission of Peter's leadership; nor is the transmission of apostolic authority in general very clear. Furthermore, the Petrine texts were subjected to differing interpretations as early as the time of the Church Fathers. Yet the church at Rome, the city in which Peter and Paul taught and were martyred, came to be recognized as possessing a unique responsibility among the churches: its bishop was seen to perform a special service in relation to the unity of the churches, and in relation to fidelity to the apostolic inheritance, thus exercising among his fellow bishops functions analogous to those ascribed to Peter, whose successor the bishop of Rome was claimed to be.[16]

Our consideration of what the New Testament says and does not say about the ministry of Peter and Paul and their relationship to the Church of Rome provides the horizon needed to evaluate the subsequent developments of the ministry of the Bishop of Rome. Believing that the Holy Spirit is guiding the Church in its journey through history, we will now turn to look at the development of the papacy from post-apostolic times to the present.

THE BISHOP OF ROME IN THE EARLY CHURCH

In responding to Pope John Paul's invitation to dialogue about the papacy, we want to express clearly the historical and theological perspective that we are using in our presentation of the history of the papacy. As the bishops of Rome found themselves called to exercise pastoral leadership in changing societal circumstances, they often responded by adopting aspects of the structures of authority and governance that were being used within contemporary secular society. They saw themselves as authorized to exercise the pastoral authority they felt was necessary in order to meet the challenges they faced in fulfilling their ministry of leadership by appealing to ever expanding interpretations of the meaning of the powers that they believed were given to Peter by Christ and, hence, to them as his successors. Although this was often done with the best of intentions in order to preserve the integrity of the faith and the welfare of the Church, at times it resulted in modes of pastoral leadership that contradicted Gospel values and did not correspond to the vision of Petrine and Pauline leadership presented in the New Testament. Throughout the history of the Church, the Holy Spirit has provided pneumatic correctives to papal misinterpretations of Petrine authority through the Pauline ministry of other bishops and prophetic voices among the clergy and the laity. The failures of the bishops of Rome over the centuries to heed the pneumatic correctives offered through the Pauline ministry has resulted in great harm to the unity of the Church and its mission of preaching the Gospel. The bishops of Rome in the 21st century are being called to listen to what the Spirit is calling them to become and to do in order to exercise their true ministry of service of unity in diversity to the universal Church by undergoing a *kenosis* that will restore the Petrine and Pauline ministries presented in the New Testament and the Early Church.

Although the monarchical episcopate was present in many of the local Churches of the Roman Empire, such as those of Antioch and Asia Minor, by the beginning of the second century, it took another fifty years before the Church of Rome moved from a presbyteral form of polity to that of a monarchical episcopate around 150. Prior to the middle of the second century there seems to have been a senior presbyter, such as Clement of Rome, within the college of presbyters who cared for the complex array of small house churches that made up the Roman Church as a whole. This original presbyteral pattern of authority fits with what we know from I Peter where the author has Peter speak of himself in 5:1 as a "fellow presbyter" (*sumpresbuteros*). The continuance of the presbyteral pattern well into the second century may represent a desire on the part of the community to preserve the memory within the Roman Church of the collegial ministry and witness of both Peter and Paul. The challenge to apostolic authority and teaching posed by the presence of various Gnostic sects in Rome may have provided the impetus to move from a presbyteral to an episcopal form of polity since bishops came to be seen in the second century not only as true successors of the apostles, but also as the voices of authentic apostolic teaching within the local Churches.

By the mid-third century the monarchical episcopate was an established reality, as we saw in Chapter 4 when we looked at the Church of Rome in 250. Pope Stephen I (254–257), in his controversy with the Church in North Africa over the question of rebaptism, seems to have been the first to have used the text of Matthew 16:18–19: "And so I say to you, you are Peter, and upon this rock I will build my church, and the gates of the netherworld shall not prevails against it. I will give you the keys to the kingdom of heaven. Whatever you bind on earth shall be bound in heaven, and whatever you loose on earth shall be loosed in heaven," as the basis for his authority to intervene in the life of another local Church. The great Church historian, Williston Walker, explains the response of the African Church to the claim of Pope Stephen in the person of Bishop Cyprian of Carthage:

> Each bishop in his place succeeded to and exercised the apostolic authority. Each bishop therefore had a right to a voice in the common concerns of the whole church, which was governed properly not by an individual but by the col-

lege of bishops itself. Even the bishop of Rome—who certainly enjoyed a special dignity and a special right to leadership, as successor to St. Peter—was nevertheless, substantively, the colleague and therefore the equal of his brethren.[17]

The position of Cyprian, which embraced the distinction between what will later be called the primacy of honor and the primacy of jurisdiction of the bishop of Rome, saw the bishop of Rome as the first among equals in the episcopal college and the sign of its unity but not as one who had the jurisdictional authority to interfere in the life or discipline of other local Churches. Cyprian's understanding of the role of the bishop of Rome in the life of the universal Church was the common understanding of the local churches of the East and also most of the local Churches of the West outside of the direct sphere of Roman influence.

In the fourth century, as we saw in Chapter 4, the bishops of the Church of the developing Christian Empire not only had spiritual authority over their own local Churches, they also participated in the civil power structures of the Empire. The position of Rome as the imperial capital and the burial place of Peter and Paul, as well as the strong role of the Bishops of Rome in defending the orthodox Christian faith by upholding the decisions of the first four Ecumenical Councils of the Church at Nicaea, I Constantinople, Ephesus and Chalcedon, contributed to the growing prestige of the papacy in the fourth and early fifth centuries.

Pope Leo I (440–461) is the symbol of the new understanding of Petrine ministry in the Church that began evolving in the fifth century. The twofold challenge to pastoral leadership that Leo I faced was 1) the growing Christological controversy over the orthodox understanding of the divinity and humanity of Christ and 2) the invasion of the Western Roman Empire by Germanic tribes from beyond the Rhine and the Danube and the resultant chaos that this had produced. The pastoral response of Leo was to see himself "as a veritable reincarnation of Peter who continued to speak and act through him."[18] He writes in Sermon III, on the anniversary of his episcopal consecration: "And so if anything is rightly done and rightly decreed by us . . .it is his work [Peter's] and merits whose power lives and authority prevails in his See."[19] Leo's *Tome to Flavian*, which presented the Western understanding of Christ as being one person in two natures, human and divine, had a significant impact on the fathers gathered at the Council of Chalcedon in 451 and, according to tradition, caused them to say that Peter had spoken through Leo. The teaching authority of Rome as a center of orthodox doctrine under Leo added to the prestige of the papacy, but it would also lead to subsequent conflicts with the Roman Emperors in the East who saw themselves as responsible for maintaining orthodoxy in the Empire. Besides believing that he was invested with the authority of Peter to maintain the apostolic faith, Leo also believed that he had Peter's authority of oversight (*episcope*) over the universal Church, having not only a primacy of honor, but also a primacy of jurisdiction, which gave him the right to intervene in the life of local churches.[20] The Eastern ecclesiology of the pentarchy, that is the Bishops of Rome, Constantinople, Alexandria, Antioch and Jerusalem, together constituting the core of communal episcopal leadership within the universal Church with the Bishop of Rome, holding the primacy of honor, could have been a Pauline pneumatic corrective of the Western understanding of the pope as having not only a primacy of honor, but also a primacy of jurisdiction, as that began to emerge under Leo. However, the Christological struggles in the East in Alexandria, Antioch and Jerusalem after Chalcedon, and the subsequent loss of these three patriarchal sees to the forces of Islam in the mid-seventh century rendered that impossible. The collapse of civil authority in many parts of the West following the Germanic invasions caused Leo and other bishops to assume civil power in order to maintain law and order in their local churches in the absence of Roman officials. Leo I's identification of Peter with the current bishop of Rome and what that could mean in terms of papal authority and power, both in the spiritual and temporal orders, would have profound ramifications for the future of the universal Church.

THE BISHOP OF ROME
IN THE EARLY AND HIGH MEDIEVAL CHURCH

The Early Middle Ages from 600–1000 are a time of great transition in which the bishops of Rome were faced with the challenges of 1) converting and civilizing the Germanic kingdoms that now ruled Western Europe and 2) dealing with the Eastern Christian Church in the Byzantine Empire from which it was increasingly alienated. Confronted by the Arian Lombards in the north and central part of Italy and the Iconoclastic Byzantine Emperors in the south of Italy, the bishops of Rome forged an alliance with the Carolingians of the Catholic Frankish kingdom in the mid-eighth century. The Franks defeated the Lombards and gave the popes the territory, which would eventually become the Papal States. In return the popes supported the Carolingians in their bid for power in the Frankish kingdom, and in 800 Pope Leo III (795–816) crowned Charlemagne as Roman Emperor of the West, the first since the deposition of Romulus Augustus in 476. The popes now had a territorial base for their temporal power and took the initiative in restoring the Roman Empire in the West. This papally created Western Empire would be short-lived because of internecine struggles within the Carolingian family and a new wave of invasions by the Vikings from the north, the Magyars from the east and the

Muslims from the south. In the midst of this new challenge to find order amidst chaos, a pope with a vision similar to that of Leo I came to be bishop of Rome, Nicholas I (858–867).

Nicholas had at his disposal two documents claiming to be from the Early Church which were in actuality forgeries: the *Donation of Constantine* created in the mid-eighth century and the *Pseudo-Isidorian Decretals* created during the mid-ninth century. The *Donation of Constantine* claimed that the fourth century Christian emperor had handed over to Pope Sylvester (314–335) all spiritual authority in the East and West and temporal power and authority in the West: ". . . we convey to the oft-mentioned and most blessed Sylvester, universal pope, . .all provinces, palaces and districts of the city of Rome and Italy and of the regions of the West."[21]

This document came to be known as a forgery only in the fifteenth century; but in the Middle Ages "this forgery did provide, at least partially, the ideological groundwork for a discontinuity of sizeable proportions regarding the pope's understanding of his role in the world. Beginning with the mid-eight century or thereabouts, the popes came to see themselves more and more as political and territorial potentates, as well as spiritual primates."[22] The *Pseudo-Isidorian Decretals or False Decretals* "attacked the intrusions of lay and royal jurisdiction into the sphere of the Church, and for the forgers, this problem seemed to be most effectively addressed by an appeal to the power of the Roman pontiff."[23] Guided by these two documents and seeing himself, like Leo I, as the living presence of Peter on earth, Nicholas I believed that "the authority of the Holy See was absolute and there was no appeal from his judgment. The papacy had, for him, the indisputable right to regulate the life of all the churches and to depose bishops without appeal. The pope was the source of the legitimacy of every law and all sacerdotal power"[24] With this understanding of papal authority, Nicholas felt that he had the right to intervene in the choice of the patriarch of Constantinople. But the Byzantine Emperor and church officials rejected his authority to interfere in the internal affairs of the life of another patriarchal see since it contradicted their deeply held vision of the pentarchy.

This growing sense of both spiritual and temporal power and authority that began in the popes of the Early Middle Ages continued to expand in the popes of the High Middle Ages and contributed to the unfortunate break between Rome and Constantinople in 1054. However, by the end of the ninth century the papacy, along with the structures of civil government, had fallen on hard times amidst the new invasions. For almost one hundred and fifty years, the papacy would become an arena in which Roman families struggled for power, and for the most part the bishops of Rome would have little to offer the Church in terms of pastoral leadership until the mid-eleventh century.

The development of feudalism sought to provide some order and protection in the midst of the societal upheavals caused by the new invasions, however, it came to have the negative aspect of investiture, the placing of church lands and appointment to church offices under the control of lay lords. The attempt to correct lay control of the church and to begin the reform of the moral and spiritual life of the church that was necessary as the new invaders began to settle down and become Christians began at the new abbey of Cluny in 910. The revival of the Western Empire that had collapsed in 887 began in the tenth century and had achieved stability in Germany and northern Italy under Henry III (1039–1056) by the mid-eleventh century. In co-operation with Abbot Hugh of Cluny, Henry III restored the moral and spiritual integrity of the papacy by removing an unworthy incumbent and appointing a holy and reform minded German bishop who became Pope Leo IX (1049–1054). Leo inaugurated a serious reform of the papacy and began addressing the moral and jurisdictional problems facing the church: simony, concubinage among the clergy and lay investiture. The work begun by Leo would find its strongest proponent among his successors in Gregory VII (1073–1085).

In responding to the pastoral challenges the church was facing, Gregory sent papal legates as agents of reform to France, England, Germany and the other nations and established a pattern of regular visits of bishops to Rome so that they could report on the state of their dioceses. In 1075 he issued a statement of his vision of papal power and authority, *Dictatus Papae*, that articulated anew the belief of his predecessors, Leo I and Nicholas I, that Peter truly lived and acted in the bishop of Rome. He drew heavily from the material in the *False Decretals,* but also emphasized his own claim to authority by proclaiming that "the Roman Church has never erred, nor ever, by the witness of Scripture, shall err to all eternity."[25] Gregory's desire to end lay investiture and his belief that he had the power to do so, and the right to depose any ruler who opposed him, led to his fateful encounter with the German Emperor Henry IV (1056–1106). Although the pope was the moral victor in the struggle, he died in exile while Henry won the battle and continued to control the appointment of bishops in the Empire and to invest them with their lands. In 1122, at the Synod of Worms, Pope Callistus II (1119–1124) and Emperor Henry V (1106 -1125) reached a settlement of the investiture controversy that tried to carefully balance the rights of lay rulers and the rights of the church. As we move into the high middle ages, we find that in defending what they believed to be the rights of the church, the popes continued to make ever greater claims to authority and power in both the spiritual and the temporal realms, while the rulers of Europe continued to resist what they believe to be unacceptable claims that undermined their own God-given authority to govern as Christian rulers.

The pastoral challenges that faced Innocent III (1198–1216) during his pontificate were related to 1) the growing awareness that European rulers had of their rights and privileges as they were rooted in law and feudal custom; 2) the expanding bureaucracy that was necessary to hear the numerous legal cases that were now being appealed to the papal court; 3) the need for new approaches to pastoral care to deal with an increasingly urbanized society that was experiencing the beginnings of the university system that would transform Europe and 4) a society that was changing because of its encounter with the Byzantine and Islamic worlds through the crusades that had been launched by Pope Urban II in 1095 to recover the Holy Land. Innocent's response to these issues came from his understanding of his role as bishop of Rome to be as Peter was: the "vicar of Christ" who was invested with the "plentitude of power." He wrote of his role as pope:

> Only St. Peter was invested with the plentitude of power. See then what manner of servant this is, appointed over the household; he is indeed the vicar of Jesus Christ, the successor of St. Peter, the Lord's anointed . . .set in the midst between God and man . . .less than God but greater than man, judging all men and judged by none.[26]

While the plentitude of power was primarily ecclesiastical in nature for Innocent, he believed that he could, when necessary for the good of Christendom, exercise temporal power as well, which he did, for example, when he released from their oaths those who had sworn allegiance to the Emperor Otto IV. Three times a week he held a consistory with his cardinals to hear legal cases that had been appealed to Rome from all over Europe. To care for the increasing number of clerics who were now serving in the Roman curia, he conferred on them the right to the revenues of the next vacant post in one of the dioceses of Christendom, thus depriving local churches of both revenues and resident ministers.[27] He approved the rule presented by St. Francis in 1210 and encouraged St. Dominic in 1215, thus setting in motion the approval of the mendicant orders that would be major agents of pastoral care in urban areas and would be directly subject to the bishop of Rome rather than the local bishop. Innocent called the Fourth Lateran Council in 1215: "to uproot vices and implant virtues, to correct abuses and reform morals, to eliminate heresies and strengthen faith, to allay differences and establish peace, to check persecutions and cherish liberty, to persuade Christian princes and people to grant succor and support for the Holy Land from both clergy and layfolk."[28] The disciplinary decrees that were passed were balanced and well designed, and if they had been consistently implemented the history of the Church might have been different, but Innocent died in the summer of 1216, six months after the close of the Council. Innocent saw the Crusade that he had supported in 1204 diverted to Constantinople. After the city had been taken and ravaged, he hoped that the establishment of a Latin patriarchate there might further reunion between Rome and Constantinople, but it only deepened the wounds that the legates of Leo IX had created in the debacle of their excommunication of the Patriarch, Michael Cerularius, in 1054. Innocent III had high principles but his understanding of the papacy led to disastrous results in the future.

THE BISHOP OF ROME IN THE LATE MIDDLE AGES, THE RENAISSANCE AND THE REFORMATION

The attempts by the thirteenth century successors of Innocent III to implement his vision of the bishop of Rome as the vicar of Christ who had the plentitude of spiritual and temporal power necessary for the oversight of Christendom, not only produced disharmony in the spiritual order because of its intrusiveness in the life of local churches, but also conflict in the temporal order because of the resistance of the rulers of Europe to what they perceived as papal infringement upon their lawful rights. At the heart of the problem was the fact that by the possession of the papal states the popes were, themselves, temporal rulers who often used their spiritual authority to achieve temporal goals. The pontificate of Boniface VIII (1294–1303) exemplifies the challenge to the vision of papal authority that the bishops of Rome were facing at the dawning of the late middle ages.

In response to the attempt of the kings of England and France to tax their clergy without papal approval, Boniface, in 1296, issues the papal bull, *Clericis laicos,* in which he stated: "That laymen have been very hostile to the clergy antiquity relates; and it is clearly proven by the present time. . . Nor do they prudently realize that power over clerics or ecclesiastical persons or goods is forbidden them."[29] In responding to the pope's bull and his threats of excommunication, Philip IV (1285–1314) of France "forbade the export of all monies and gold from France to the Papal States—thus cutting off a large portion of the pope's regular revenues almost overnight."[30] This action caused Boniface to back down temporarily and allow the king to tax the clergy, but in 1302 he issued the bull *Unam Sanctam* in which he declared that temporal authority is subject to the spiritual power and concluded by saying: "it is altogether necessary to salvation for every human creature to be subject to the Roman pontiff."[31] Philip responded in 1303 by sending his chief minister, William Nogaret to take Boniface captive. Although the pontiff was eventually rescued by the people of Anagni, where he was temporarily in residence, the traumatic effects of the physical and psychological violence that he had experienced at the hands of Nogaret eventuated in his death a few weeks later. The struggle between Boniface and Philip was the prelude to the dark night that would envelop the papacy for more than a hundred years.

Under the influence of Philip IV, Clement V (1305–1314), who was elected pope in 1309, moved the papal court to Avignon, where it would remain for seventy years under seven French popes. William La Due offers an important observation: "The Avignon papacy, with its luxurious lifestyle and exploding bureaucracy, multiplied almost beyond counting the financial demands on the various dioceses, chapters, parishes, monasteries, and religious houses all over Western Christendom . . . This escalated the general unrest and notably increased the level of frustration everywhere."[32] The hope of a new beginning that was raised when Gregory XI returned the papacy to Rome in 1377 was quickly dashed when the cardinals who chose his successor, Urban VI (1378–1389), a few months later elected a second pope, Clement VII (1378–1394), and thus began the Great Schism. The attempts to end the schism proved fruitless and by 1409 there were three popes, one in Rome, one in Avignon and one in Pisa.

The leadership of Emperor Sigismund (1410–1437) effected the gathering of the Council of Constance (1414–1418) which would finally end the schism and elect a new pope, Martin V (1417–1431). The Council clearly enunciated an ecclesial vision which could have served as a pneumatic corrective to a papal vision that had become more concerned with serving its own political and economic needs rather than meeting the pastoral needs of the universal Church:

> It declares that, legitimately assembled in the Holy Spirit, constituting a general council and representing the Catholic Church militant, it has power immediately from Christ, and that everyone of whatever state or dignity, even papal, is bound to obey it in these matters which pertain to the faith, the eradication of the said schism and the general reform of the Church of God in head and members.[33]

The pastoral challenge that faced Martin V was to inaugurate the process of holding general councils on a regular basis that would work with the pope in the reform of the church in head and members. However, Martin and his fifteenth century papal successors were absolutely opposed to the ecclesial vision of the conciliarists. The popes managed to negate the plan for regular councils and to return the church to the monarchical vision of their thirteenth and fourteenth century predecessors. But the failure to enter upon the program of reform envisioned by the Council of Constance was to have serious consequences for the future, as La Due indicates:

> The last half of the fifteenth century witnesses the rise of the Renaissance popes, who proceeded to shrink the office down to the size and shape of a regional Italian duchy, whose lord and ruler manifested less and less interest in the wider concerns of the Christian world. The stage was now set for the cataclysmic Protestant Revolt.[34]

Clement VII (1523–1534), the last of the Renaissance popes, refused to heed the call to summon a general council to deal with the ever growing Protestant Reformation that was spreading all over Europe. Nor did he engage in any effective reform of the Roman Church. He seemed to believe that the unity of the Church would be restored by political and military means. He was sorely mistaken and represents the inability of the Renaissance popes to provide the kind of pastoral leadership sorely needed by Europe on the threshold of the modern world.

THE BISHOP OF ROME
FROM THE COUNCIL OF TRENT TO VATICAN I

The countless voices for the reform of the Church in head and members in the sixteenth century offered the Renaissance popes a pneumatic corrective that could have averted the terrible tragedy of the religious divisions within Western Christendom that we are still trying to heal. However, the bishops of Rome waited almost twenty five years to call the Council of Trent after the beginnings of the Reformation, and it took almost twenty five more years before the Council completed its work and the implementation of the reforms began. As La Due comments:

> Many of the popes understood the roots of the problems and the underlying corruption of the Roman system for centuries before the revolt, but even the strongest and most resolute of them, like Innocent III, were not up to enforcing the necessary changes.[35]

Pius V (1566–1572), the first pope after the completion of the Council, was both a saint and man determined to face the pastoral challenge to implement the decrees of Trent. Because the Council chose not to address issues surrounding papal primacy, the monarchical vision of the ministry of the bishop of Rome remained firmly in place. However, the Council did try to strengthen the role of bishops in the oversight of their dioceses. Pius V sought to renew the episcopacy by the appointment of reform minded bishops and encouraged the establishment of seminaries for the education of priests. He oversaw the publication of the Roman Catechism in 1566, a revision of the Roman Breviary in 1568 and a revision of the Roman missal in 1570. His successor, Gregory XIII (1572–1585) continued the work he began and used nuncios and legates as liaisons with the Catholic kings to encourage them to implement the decrees and directives of Trent. The third of the Post-Tridentine reforming popes, Sixtus V (1585–1590), reorganized the Curia and sought to put the Papal States on a sound financial basis La Due offers this summary of the results of their efforts at reforming the Church in accord with the decrees of Trent:

> Pius V, Gregory XIII, and Sixtus V had initiated a centralization of church rule which has survived to this day. Their enforcement of the reforms of Trent—in some cases through an episcopate with widely augmented powers and in other cases through the papal nuncios—served as the foundation for this development. Liturgy, discipline, and theology were rendered more uniform which to some extent was good, but uniformity often blurs the richness of diversity. This was the state at the of the Church at the close of the sixteenth century.[36]

The momentum of reform began to slow down at the beginning of the seventeenth century and the authority of the popes diminished in the face of the growing power of the Catholic absolutist monarchs, as La Due indicates:

> The seventeenth and eighteenth centuries were not memorable ones for the Roman pontiffs, who fell under the control of the kings of Spain, France and the Hapsburg Empire. Clement XI's imprecise bull, *Unigenitus* (1713), precipitated a heated discussion on the irreformable character of the popes' teaching authority which would not be put to rest until Vatican I.[37]

The struggle of the popes to exercise their universal ministry of pastoral oversight took a whole new turn at the end of the eighteenth century with the French Revolution and Napoleon.

Pope Pius VII (1800–1823) faced the pastoral challenge of trying to restore and renew the Church amidst the havoc wrought first by the French Revolution and then Napoleon. His pastoral response to the complexities of church-state relations was to negotiate concordats with civil rulers that protected the freedom of the Church to carry on its life and ministry. Although Napoleon violated the spirit of the Concordat of 1801 and eventually occupied the Papal States bringing Pius to France as a prisoner in 1809, the pope bore his imprisonment with courage and after his release offered his fallen persecutor's relatives refuge in Rome. In 1814 Pius VII restored the Society of Jesus that had been suppressed by his predecessor, Clement XIV in 1773 under pressure from the kings of Portugal, Spain and France. Besides his constant efforts at rebuilding a devastated Church in many parts of Europe, the pope had to face the question of the future of the Papal States. While they had been restored to the papacy by the Congress of Vienna in 1815, they were in a state of turmoil because of the growing desire for the unification of Italy under its own civilian government. Because Pius and his nineteenth century successors saw the Papal States as part of the Patrimony of Peter entrusted to their care, they resisted the unification movement. Unfortunately, the only way that they could maintain control of the Papal States, as the desire for a united Italy gained momentum, was through the use of foreign troops supplied by France and Austria. This situation seriously endangered the spiritual mission of the Church and profoundly conditioned the way in which nineteenth century popes would come to view the modern world. The turmoil in Italy continued to worsen under the successors of Pius VII, Leo XII (1823–1829), Pius VIII (1829–1830) Gregory XVI (1831–1846) and Pius IX (1846–1878).

The struggle between the leaders of the Italian *Resorgimento* and the papacy reached its denouement in 1870 while the First Vatican Council, called by Pius IX, was in session.

THE BISHOP OF ROME FROM VATICAN I TO VATICAN II

From his perspective as bishop of Rome responsible for the universal Church, the challenge facing Pius IX was how to maintain the apostolic faith and Christian life in a world where the traditional teachings of the faith were being questioned by contemporary biblical scholarship and historical studies and where the moral values of the Gospel were being undermined by rationalism and secularism. For the pope, the attempt of Italian nationalists to dismantle the Papal States, that had been the source of the Church's temporal power and freedom to fulfill its mission since the eighth century, was the symbol of the unbelief and the innovations of the modern world they were attempting to overthrow the teaching and authority of the Catholic Church. His response was to strive to maintain control of the Papal states, to condemn all contemporary outlooks that seemed contrary to the traditional teaching of the Church in the *Syllabus of Errors* and to call the First Vatican Council to reaffirm papal authority as a way of protecting the Church from the doctrinal and moral errors of the modern world. The attempt to preserve the Papal States was a failure and only increased anti-clerical feelings towards the Church. Pius IX concluded the *Syllabus of Errors* in 1864 by saying that it is an error that: "The Roman Pontiff can and should reconcile and harmonize himself with progress, with liberalism and with recent civilization."[38] The First Vatican Council (1869–1870) never finished its agenda because the departure of the French garrison in the summer of 1870 left Rome vulnerable to the occupation of Italian troops, but the Dogmatic Constitution, *Pastor Aeternus,* which was approved on July 18, 1870, was to be a truly defining moment in the unfolding understanding of the ministry of the bishop of Rome.

In its treatment of papal primacy *Pastor Aeternus* described the jurisdiction of the bishop of Rome, as the successor of St. Peter, over all the dioceses of the Catholic world as being "immediate" and "ordinary." Later in the document, as La Due indicates:

Papal infallibility was described as a personal gift belonging to the pontiff. It is separate from the infallibility enjoyed by the whole body of bishops joined with the pope. Although the cooperation and council of the Church are not ruled out, they are not required for the valid use of the papal prerogative. Further, the pope must speak *ex cathedra*, i.e. as supreme pastor and teacher of all Christians, and he must intend to teach a doctrine pertaining to faith or morals to be held by the whole Church. Finally, the object of papal infallibility extends only as far as the infallibility of the Church, and no further.[39]

The legacy of Pius IX was a Church fearful of the modern world and centered on the papacy as the absolute source of jurisdictional and teaching authority in the Church.

Leo XIII (1878–1903) had a more positive view of the modern world. In his many encyclicals he sought to address the complex social issues the Church was facing with wisdom and pastoral sensitivity, but he continued the policy of Pius IX of centralizing the Church under the papacy. Pius X (1903–1914) was a man of deep personal holiness who, like his predecessor Pius IX, was fearful of contemporary developments in biblical, historical and theological studies, and he tried to protect the integrity of the faith from what he considered aberrations by his condemnation of Catholic theologians with modernist tendencies. Benedict XV (1914–1922) guided the Church through the difficult days of World War I and codified the ecclesial vision of the ministry of the bishop of Rome from Vatican I in the new *Code of Canon Law* he promulgated in 1918. Through his careful diplomacy, Pius XI (1922–1939) negotiated the Lateran Treaty of 1929 with Benito Mussolini which settled the Roman Question of the papal states and recognized the pope "as the civil ruler of the tiny Vatican state (109 acres) and accorded all the rights that his political sovereignty required."[40]

The pastoral challenge faced by Pope Pius XII (1939–1958) was to guide the Church through World War II and the rebuilding of the post-war period. His response to these tasks was guided by his high monarchical vision of the office of the bishop of Rome. He was deeply committed to the teaching dimension of the Petrine office and his great encyclicals, *Mystici Corporis* (1943), on the Church as the body of Christ, *Divino afflante Spiritu* (1943), on biblical scholarship, and *Mediator Dei* (1947), on the liturgy, helped to lay the foundation for the subsequent work of Vatican II. However, he became more cautious by 1950 and his criticism of the "New Theology" coming out of France in the writings of men such as Congar, Chenu and De Lubac indicated a shift toward a more conservative approach in his theology. In 1950 he defined the Assumption of Mary as a dogma of the Catholic faith and caused great consternation among Orthodox Christians because he was "amplifying Christian doctrine without consulting the eastern churches" and among

Protestant Christians because the dogma did not seem to have a solid foundation in the New Testament.[41] Pius XII seemed to have no real commitment to the ecumenical movement in general and was not interested in the first assembly of the World Council of Churches held in Amsterdam in 1948 or the second assembly held in Evanston in 1954.[42] The Roman Catholic Church of the mid-twentieth century saw itself as a world of its own, with parishes, educational institutions and social service agencies that trained and cared for the faithful so that they could live good lives in a world that was either indifferent or hostile to the faith and values of the Church. This would change with Pope John XXIII.

THE BISHOP OF ROME FROM VATICAN II TO THE PRESENT

On January 25, 1959, a few months after his election as bishop of Rome, John XXIII announced his intention to convene the Second Vatican Council. At the opening of the Council on October 11, 1962 he spoke of the need for the Church to bring herself up to date and set forth his horizon of understanding for the challenge that must be faced:

> The substance of the ancient doctrine or the deposit of the faith is one thing and the way in which it is presented is another. And it is the latter that must be taken into great consideration with patience if necessary, everything being measured in the forms and proportions of a magisterium which is predominately pastoral in character.[43]

During the first session of the Second Vatican Council in the Fall of 1962 no documents were approved, but serious discussions were held on the documents on liturgy, revelation, social communication, the Church and the Eastern Churches. On June 3, 1963, between the first and the second sessions of the Council, Pope John XXIII died, leaving to his successors the continuation of the work of reform and renewal of the Church that he had begun so courageously.

When Pope Paul VI opened the second session of the Council in the Fall of 1963, he gave the *Constitution on the Church* priority over all the other documents under consideration. In their work the fathers of the Council tried to place the papal prerogatives articulated at Vatican I in the context of the college of bishops and papal infallibility in the context of the inerrancy of the Church.[44] Their attempt to balance papal authority with the episcopal authority of the college of bishops was muted by the *Prefatory Note* that was added at the direction of Paul VI indicating that the care of the universal Church is "the pope's proper responsibility which he can freely choose to exercise either individually or collegially at his own discretion."[45] At the end of the second session the Council issued the *Constitution on the Liturgy,* and at the end of the third session, in 1964, issued the *Constitution on the Church.* In the fourth and final session, in 1965, the Council issued the last two of its major documents, the *Constitution on Divine Revelation* and the *Constitution on the Church in the Modern World.* Paul VI's goal in the implementation of the Council was to initiate dialogue within the Church and in the modern world. Unfortunately, his attempts at dialogue were not very successful as the uproar over his encyclical *Humanae Vitae,* on birth control and contraception, and the dissatisfaction over the agendas of the newly created synod of bishops clearly indicate. To his lasting credit, however, he did open up conversations with the Eastern Orthodox and set the stage for the work of his successor, Pope John Paul II, in ecumenical dialogue.

The impact of the Petrine ministry of John Paul II was very significant within the Church and in the world. The codification of the work of Vatican II in the 1983 *Code of Canon Law,* the 1992 and 1997 editions of the *Catechism of the Catholic Church,* and his numerous encyclicals and letters stand as witness to the seriousness with which he approached the teaching dimension of the Petrine office in the spirit of his predecessor, Pius XII. His approach to the synods of bishops were more successful than that of his predecessor, Paul VI. His role in helping to free the nations of Eastern Europe from Communism, his papal visits to all parts of the world and his deep commitment to ecumenical dialogue indicated his desire to be a universal pastor who was concerned not only about the Roman Catholic Church, but also about Christina unity and the values of freedom, justice and peace in the world. John Paul II profoundly influenced the development of the Petrine ministry. The Church and world now await the next chapter in the history of the papacy to be written by Pope Benedict XVI.

CONCLUSION

In asking ourselves what is the Spirit saying to the Churches at the beginning of the 21st century, amidst the search for Christian unity, we have explored the ministry and mission of servant-leaders in Chapter 4, and the development of the ministry of the bishop of Rome from Peter to John Paul II in Chapter 5. It is clear, as Pope John Paul II noted in *Ut Unum Sint,* that we are at a critical moment in the ministry of servant leaders in the Church and in the ministry of the bishop of Rome as the servant of the servants of God unto unity in diversity:

When the Catholic Church affirms that office of the bishop of Rome corresponds to the will of Christ, she does not separate his office from the mission entrusted to the whole body of bishops, who are also "vicars and ambassadors of Christ." The bishop of Rome is a member of the "college," and the bishops are his brothers in the ministry. Whatever relates to the unity of all Christian communities clearly forms part of the concerns of the primacy. As bishop of Rome I am fully aware, as I have reaffirmed in the present encyclical letter, that Christ ardently desires the full and visible communion of all those communities in which by virtue of God's faithfulness, His Spirit dwells. I am convinced that I have a particular responsibility in this regard, above all in acknowledging the ecumenical aspirations of the majority of the Christian communities and in heeding the request made of me to find a way of exercising the primacy which,while in no way renouncing what is essential to its mission, is nonetheless open to a new situation.[46]

With the material on the history of the development of the Petrine ministry as background, we can now try to respond, in the next chapter, to Pope John Paul II's desire of finding a way of exercising the primacy of the pope in the new situation in which we find ourselves by offering our observations on the *kenosis* to which the bishop of Rome, as the servant of the servants of God unto unity in diversity, is being called by the Holy Spirit through the Churches.

NOTES

1. Pope John Paul II, "*Ut Unum Sint,*" *Origins* 25:4 (1995), 52.

2. Pope John Paul II, "*Ut Unum Sint,*" *Origins* 25:4:70.

3. Pope John Paul II, "*Ut Unum Sint,*" *Origins* 25:4:70.

4. Pope John Paul II, "*Ut Unum Sint,*" *Origins* 25: 4: 90.

5. Oscar Cullmann, *Peter, Disciple, Apostle, Martyr* (New York: Meridian Books, 1953), 30.

6. Cullmann, *Peter*, 32–33.

7. Cullmann, *Peter*, 55.

8. Cullmann, *Peter*, 152.

9. *History of Eusebius*, 2:22:2.

10. *St. Clement of Rome and St. Ignatius of Antioch, Ancient Christian Writers,* trans. James Kleist (Westminister, Maryland: Newman Books, 1946), 12.

11. Cullmann, *Peter*, 101–102.

12. Cullmann, *Peter*, 211–212.

13. Cullmann, *Peter*, 223.

14. Cullmann, *Peter*, 219–220.

15. Cullmann, *Peter*, 229.

16. Anglican-Roman Catholic International Commission, *The Final Report, September 1981—Authority in the Church II* (London: SPCK, 1982), 83–84.

17. Williston Walker, Richard A. Norris, David W. Lotz, and Robert T. Handy, *A History of the Christian Church* (4th Edition) (New York: Macmillan Publishing Co., 1985), 83.

18. William J. La Due, *The Chair of Saint Peter: A History of the Papacy* (Maryknoll, New York: Orbis Books, 1999), 50.

19. La Due, *The Chair of Saint Peter*, 50.

20. La Due, *The Chair of St. Peter*, 291–292.

21. La Due, *The Chair of St.* Peter, 75.

22. La Due, *The Chair of St. Peter*, 75.

23. La Due, *The Chair of St. Peter*, 86.

24. La Due, *The Chair of St. Peter*, 86.

25. La Due, *The Chair of St. Peter*, 100.

26. La Due, *The Chair of St. Peter*, 119.

27. La Due, *The Chair of St. Peter*, 121.

28. La Due, *The Chair of St. Peter*, 122.

29. La Due, *The Chair of St. Peter*, 136.

30. La Due, *The Chair of St. Peter*, 137.

31. La Due, *The Chair of St. Peter*, 138.

32. La Due, *The Chair of St. Peter*, 181.

33. La Due, *The Chair of St. Peter*, 162

34. La Due, *The Chair of St. Peter*, 181–182.

35. La Due, *The Chair of St. Peter*, 201.

36. La Due, *The Chair of St. Peter*, 207.

37. La Due, *The Chair of St. Peter*, 239.

38. La Due, *The Chair of St. Peter*, 237.

39. La Due, *The Chair of St. Peter*, 245.

40. La Due, *The Chair of St. Peter*, 258

41. La Due, *The Chair of St. Peter*, 263.

42. La Due, *The Chair of St. Peter*, 263.

43. La Due, *The Chair of St. Peter*, 265.

44. La Due, *The Chair of St. Peter*, 267–268,

45. La Due, *The Chair of St. Peter*, 269.

46. Pope John Paul II, "*Ut Unum Sint*," *Origins* 25:4: 69.

Chapter Six

Authority as the
Service of Unity in Diversity

INTRODUCTION

A burning issue facing all Christians at the beginning of the 21st century is how to heal the scandal of the divisions within Christianity, divisions that are contrary to Christ's will for his Church to be the sacrament of unity and are harmful to the proclamation of the Gospel. The Holy Spirit is calling the churches to move beyond our divisions and to find anew the unity in diversity that is meant to be the sacramental reality of the one, holy, catholic and apostolic Church.

Pope John Paul II, in his encyclical letter *Ut Unum Sint*, recognized the responsibility that the Roman Catholic Church in general and the bishop of Rome in particular have to work toward the restoration of Christian unity. The numerous ecumenical dialogues between Christians of the East and West over the past forty years bear witness to the desire to move forward together toward the unity in diversity that we all seek as disciples of the crucified and risen Lord. The kind of leadership that the bishop of Rome must provide in order to move the dialogues toward Christian unity forward will call for a profound *kenosis* within the Roman Catholic Church and will require a new openness to the mystery of Peter: disciple, apostle and martyr. The Petrine ministry cannot be about power as it is exercised in the structures of civil society, but rather, if it is to be in accord with the Gospel, it must be an apostolic witness to *kenotic* service that brings unity in diversity to the Church by sharing in the paschal mystery of the crucified and risen Lord.

In this chapter we shall explore the question of authority in the Church because it is one of the central issues that have divided Christians in the East and West for centuries. Using the *Catechism of the Catholic Church* and the documents on authority from the Anglican-Roman Catholic International Commission (ARCIC), we shall consider authority in the Church in five areas: 1) scripture and tradition; 2) the laity; 3) episcopacy and synodality; 4) primacy and conciliarity; 5) teaching authority.

THE AUTHORITY OF SCRIPTURE AND TRADITION

The Second Edition of the *Catechism of the Catholic Church* summarizes the understanding of the Roman Catholic Church regarding the authority of scripture and tradition and their mutual interrelationship as it is presented in the *Dogmatic Constitution on Divine Revelation (Dei Verbum)* from the Second Vatican Council:

> Christ the Lord, in whom the entire Revelation of the most high God is summed up, commanded the apostles to preach the Gospel, which had been promised beforehand by the prophets, and which he fulfilled in his own person and promulgated with his own lips. In preaching the Gospel, they were to communicate the gifts of God to all men. This Gospel was to be the source of all saving truth and moral discipline. In keeping with the Lord's command the Gospel was handed on in two ways: 1) *orally* by the apostles who handed on, by the spoken word of their preaching, by the example they gave, by the institutions they established, what they themselves received—whether from the lips of Christ, from his way of life and his works, or whether they had learned it at the prompting of the Holy Spirit; 2) *in writing* by those apostles and other men associated with the apostles who, under the inspiration of the same Holy Spirit, committed the message of salvation to writing. In order that the full and living Gospel might always be preserved in the Church the apostles left bishops as their successors. They gave them their own position of teaching authority. Indeed, the apostolic preaching, which is preserved in a special way in the inspired books, was to be preserved in a continuous line of succession until the end of time. This living transmission, accomplished in the Holy Spirit, is called Tradition, since it is distinct from Sacred Scripture, though closely connected to it. Through Tradition, the Church in her doctrine, life and worship perpetuates and transmits to every generation all she herself is, all that she believes. The sayings of the holy Fathers are a witness to the life-giving presence of this Tradition, showing how its riches are poured out in the practice and life of the Church, in her belief and prayer.[1]

The *Catechism* then goes on to distinguish carefully the Apostolic Tradition, which has been described in the citation above, from ecclesial traditions.

> The Tradition here in question comes from the apostles and hands on whatever they received from Jesus' teaching and example and what they learned from the

Holy Spirit. The first generation of Christians did not yet have a written New Testament, and the New Testament itself demonstrates the process of living Tradition. Tradition is to be distinguished from the various theological, disciplinary, liturgical, or devotional traditions, born in the local churches over times. These are particular forms, adapted to different places and times, in which the great Tradition is expressed. In the light of Tradition, these traditions can be retained, modified or even abandoned under the guidance of the Church's magisterium.[2]

Understanding the difference between the Apostolic Tradition and the ecclesial traditions is crucial in continuing the reform and renewal of the Roman Catholic Church and in moving forward in the search for Christian unity.

The 1999 statement agreed upon by the Second Anglican-Roman Catholic International Commission (ARCIC II), *The Gift of Authority: Authority in the Church III*, expresses the mutual understanding that became possible through dialogue between Roman Catholic and Anglican theologians on various facets of authority in the Church. In regard to the Apostolic Tradition the statement says:

> Tradition is a dynamic process, communicating to each generation what was delivered once for all to the apostolic community. . . The Church receives, and must hand on, all those elements that are constitutive of ecclesial communion: baptism, confession of the apostolic faith, celebration of the Eucharist, and leadership by an apostolic ministry.[3]

Confession of the apostolic faith as it is found in the New Testament, the sacraments of baptism and Eucharist and the apostolic ministry are the core elements of the Christian Tradition. Because the creation of the Apostolic Tradition is the work of the Holy Spirit, its handing on is also the work of the Holy Spirit. It is a dynamic process at work in history, gathering each successive generation into the one, holy, catholic and apostolic Church. Each generation of Christians is called to receive the Apostolic Tradition as a new gift of the Holy Spirit enabling them to respond faithfully in meeting the needs of the life and growth of the Pilgrim Church as it moves through history. As the agreed statement indicates:

> The process of tradition entails the constant and perpetual reception and communication of the revealed Word of God in many varied circumstances and continually changing times. The Church's "Amen" to apostolic Tradition is a fruit of the Spirit who constantly guides the disciples into all the truth; that is, into Christ who is the way, the truth and the life (cf John 16.13; 14.6). Tradition expresses the apostolicity of the Church. What the apostles received and proclaimed is preached and the sacraments of Christ celebrated in the power of the Holy Spirit. The churches today are committed to receiving the one living apostolic Tradition, to ordering their life according to it, and transmitting it in such a way that the

Christ who comes in glory will find the people of God confessing and living the faith once for all entrusted to the saints (cf. Jude 3). Tradition makes the witness of the apostolic community present in the Church today through its corporate *memory*. Through the proclamation of the Word and the celebration of the sacraments the Holy Spirit opens the hearts of believers and manifests the Risen Lord to them. . .The purpose of Tradition is fulfilled when, through the Spirit, the Word is received and lived out in faith and hope. The witness of proclamation, sacraments and life in communion is at one and the same time the content of Tradition and its result. Thus memory bears fruit in the faithful life of believers within the communion of their local church.[4]

The authority of Scripture and Tradition is the authority of Christ ever speaking anew the message of salvation, but speaking it through the ongoing work of the Holy Spirit in ways that are meaningful to the diverse cultures in which the Church finds itself. Since it is the men and women within the communion of their local church who are called to receive anew the truth of the apostolic Tradition through the Holy Spirit and who are empowered by the celebration of word and sacrament to witness their faith in daily life, we must now turn to a consideration of the authority of the laity to serve the unity in diversity of their communities and to be agents of societal transformation.

THE AUTHORITY OF THE LAITY

The *Catechism of the Catholic Church* offers us an ecclesial vision of the laity:

The faithful, who by Baptism are incorporated into Christ and integrated into the People of God, are made sharers in their particular way in the priestly, prophetic, and kingly office of Christ, and have their own part to play in the mission of the whole Christian people in the Church and in the world.[5]

By baptism the lay faithful are joined to the crucified and risen Christ and receive His outpouring of the Holy Spirit, Who empowers them with the gifts necessary to exercise authority as service in their ministries and in their mission to proclaim the Gospel. The *Catechism* says:

Since, like all the faithful, lay Christians are entrusted by God with the apostolate by virtue of their Baptism and Confirmation, they have the right and duty, individually or grouped in associations, to work so that the divine message of salvation may be known and accepted by all throughout the earth. This duty is the more pressing when it is only through them that others can hear the Gospel and know Christ. Their activity in ecclesial communities is so necessary that, for the most part, the apostolate of the pastors cannot be fully effective without it.[6]

The declining numbers of religious and priests in the local churches of Europe and North America and the pastoral and missionary needs of the local churches in South America, Asia, Africa and Oceania make very clear how necessary it is that lay men and women take up the ministries that are theirs by baptism and that ecclesiastical leaders recognize the gifts given to the laity by the Holy Spirit which empowers them to fulfill the Church's mission in the 21st century. In trying to understand the many ways in which lay men and women may be asked to serve the church in the future we must consider the questions of a celibate priesthood and the ordination of women. The decline in vocations to the priesthood in many local churches may be seen as a pneumatic corrective to remind the Roman Church that celibacy is a gift distinct from the priesthood and that we need to return to the discipline of the apostolic church maintained by the churches of the East and the Protestant churches, which permit married presbyters. Paul reminds us: "Do we not have the right to take along a Christian wife, as do the rest of the apostles, and the brothers of the Lord, and Kephas?" (I Cor. 9:5). We shall consider the question of the ordination of women at a later point in this chapter when we discuss primacy and conciliarity.

In speaking of the participation of lay men and women in the prophetic office, the *Catechism* says:

> Christ . . . fulfills his prophetic office, not only by the hierarchy . . . but also by the laity. He accordingly both establishes them as witnesses and provides them with the sense of the faith [*sensus fidelium*] and the grace of the word. To teach in order to lead others to faith is the task of every preacher and of each believer. Lay people also fulfill their prophetic mission by evangelization, "that is, the proclamation of Christ by word and the testimony of life" . . . Lay people who are capable and trained may also collaborate in catechetical formation, in teaching the sacred sciences, and in the use of communication media. "In accord with the knowledge, competence, and preeminence which they possess, [lay persons] have the right and even at times a duty to manifest to the sacred pastors their opinion on matters which pertain to the good of the Church, and they have a right to make their opinion known to the other Christian faithful, with due regard to the integrity of the faith and morals and reverence toward their pastors, and with consideration for the common good and the dignity of persons."[7]

As indicated in Chapter 1, we need to move much further than we have in restoring the prophetic ministry of the laity that we find in the New Testament and in the history of the Church. The *consensus fidelium,* as an expression of the laity's sharing in the prophetic ministry of Christ, is meant to serve as a pneumatic corrective that constantly renews the call of the whole People of God to be the sacrament of unity and reconciliation that the Church is meant to be. We have barely begun to establish adequate structures of dialogue at the parish level, at the level of the local church, and at the level of the universal Church, where lay men and women can enter into Spirit-filled dialogue with their pastors. Such dialogue is necessary for the spiritual and temporal well being of the Church if it is to truly become the body of Christ.

The *Catechism* recognizes the crucial role of the laity in the life and ministry of the Church and the need for the development of structures of dialogue, planning and governance, where laity and clergy are mutually engaged in the exercise of their respective gifts of authority. In its treatment of the participation of the laity in Christ's kingly office, it says:

> The laity can also feel called, or be in fact called, to cooperate with their pastors in the service of the ecclesial community, for the sake of its growth and life. This can be done through the exercise of different kinds of ministries according to the grace and charisms which the Lord has been pleased to bestow on them." In the Church, "lay members of the Christian faithful can cooperate in the exercise of this power [of governance] at particular councils, diocesan synods, pastoral councils; the exercise of the pastoral care of a parish, collaboration in finance committees, and participation in ecclesiastical tribunals, etc.[8]

In Chapters 1, 2, and 3 we saw that the charisms and graces given in Baptism, Confirmation and Eucharist empower lay men and women to share in the kingly mission of Christ both within the internal life of the Church and in the transformation of society. The realization of the pneumatic potential present within the Christian community will call all of us to conversion, so that we can experience the meaning of Christian ministry and mission in new ways. As we have seen in Chapter 2, it will also require a new way of looking at the celebration of the Sunday Eucharist in general and preaching in particular, so that the gathering of a Christian community around word and sacrament is a weekly call to transformation in life and ministry together.

The Gift of Authority envisions the authority of the laity to serve the building up of the Christian community and the proclamation of the Gospel in society as flowing from a constant re-reception of the apostolic Tradition:

> Throughout the centuries the Church receives and acknowledges as a gracious gift from God all that it recognizes as a true expression of the Tradition which has been once for all delivered to the apostles. The reception is at one and the same time an act of faithfulness and of freedom. The Church must continue faithful so that the Christ who comes in glory will recognize in the Church the community he founded; it must continue to be free to receive the apostolic Tradition in new ways according to the situation by which it is confronted. The Church has the responsibility to hand on the whole apostolic Tradition, even though there may be parts which it finds hard to integrate in its life and worship.

It may be that what was of great significance for an earlier generation will again be important in the future, though its importance is not clear in the present.[9]

The Christian community of each generation is called to receive the apostolic Tradition anew through the assistance of the Holy Spirit because of the changing needs of the Church in diverse cultural situations and also because the Church as a community of frail human beings is always in need of reform:

> Within the Church the memory of the people of God may be affected or even distorted by human finitude and sin. Even though promised the assistance of the Holy Spirit, the churches from time to time lose aspects of the apostolic Tradition, failing to discern the full vision of the kingdom of God in the light of which we seek to follow Christ. The churches suffer when some element of ecclesial communion has been forgotten, neglected or abused. Fresh recourse to Tradition in a new situation is the means by which God's revelation in Christ is recalled. This is assisted by the insights of biblical scholars and theologians and the wisdom of holy persons. Thus, there may be a rediscovery of elements that were neglected and a fresh remembrance of the promises of God, leading to renewal of the Church's "Amen." There may also be a sifting of what has been received because some of the formulations of the Tradition are seen to be inadequate or even misleading in a new context. This whole process may be termed re-reception.[10]

At the beginning of the 21st century, we find ourselves being asked anew by the Holy Spirit to recover the vision of Spirit-filled Christian communities in which the pneumatic gifts of lay men and women are fully appreciated by the clergy and the authority of the laity to serve the mission of the Church as full sharers in ministry with the clergy is once more the life-giving reality for all that it was in the apostolic communities of the New Testament:

> In each community there is an exchange, a mutual give-and-take in which bishops, clergy and lay people receive from as well as give to others within the whole body. In every Christian who is seeking to be faithful to Christ and is fully incorporated into the life of the Church, there is a *sensus fidei*. This *sensus fidei* may be described as an active capacity for spiritual discernment, an intuition that is formed by worshiping and living in communion as a faithful member of the Church. When this capacity is exercised in concert by the body we may speak of the exercise of the *sensus fidelium*. The exercise of the *sensus fidei* by each member of the Church contributes to the formation of the *senus fidelium* through which the Church as a whole remains faithful to Christ. By the *sensus fidelium* the whole body contributes to, receives from and treasures the ministry of those within the community who exercise *episcope*, watching over the living memory of the Church.[11]

The gifts of the laity and the clergy are complementary. Together they build up the body of Christ and through the diversity of their ministries the Holy

Spirit preserves the apostolic Tradition. *Sensus fidelium* and *episcope* are diverse ways of exercising evangelical authority at the service of unity amidst diversity. They enable the Church to be the sacrament of Christ's reconciling presence in the world.

THE AUTHORITY OF EPISCOPACY AND SYNODALITY

The *Catechism* describes the Roman Catholic Church's understanding of the origin of episcopal authority and its collegial dimension:

> When Christ instituted the Twelve, "He constituted [them] in the form of a college or permanent assembly, at the head of which he placed Peter, chosen from among them." Just as "by the Lord's institution, St. Peter and the rest of the apostles constitute a single apostolic college, so in like fashion the Roman Pontiff, Peter's successor, and the bishops, the successors of the apostles, are related with and united to one another." The Lord made Simon, whom he named Peter, the "rock" of his Church. He gave him the keys of his Church and instituted him shepherd of the whole flock. "The office of binding and loosing which was given to Peter was also assigned to the college of apostles united to its head." This pastoral office of Peter and the other apostles belongs to the Church's very foundation and is continued by the bishops under the primacy of the Pope.[12]

Having presented the Roman Catholic Church's understanding of the parallel between Peter and the apostles and the Pope and the bishops of the Church, the *Catechism* then delineates more precisely its view of the relationship between the bishop of Rome and the college of bishops of the local churches throughout the world in terms of authority:

> The *college or body of bishops* has no authority unless united with the Roman pontiff, Peter's successor, as its head. As such, this college has "supreme and and full authority over the universal Church; but this power cannot be exercised without the agreement of the Roman Pontiff." "The College of bishops exercises power over the universal Church in a solemn manner in an ecumenical council." But "there never is an ecumenical council which is not confirmed or at least recognized as such by Peter's successor." "This college, in so far as it is composed of many members is the expression of the variety and universality of the People of God; and of the unity of the flock of Christ, in so far as it is assembled under one head."[13]

The *Catechism* then goes on to speak about the authority of the bishops in their own local churches and offers examples of episcopal synodality:

The individual *bishops* are the visible source and foundation of unity in their own particular Churches. As such, they "exercise their pastoral office over the portion of the People of God assigned to them," assisted by priests and deacons. But, as a member of the episcopal college, each bishop shares in the concern for all the Churches. The bishops exercise this care first "by ruling well their own churches as portions of the universal Church," and so contributing "to the welfare of the whole Mystical Body, which, from another point of view, is a corporate body of Churches." They extend it especially to the poor, to those persecuted for the faith, as well as to missionaries who are working throughout the world. Neighboring particular Churches who share the same culture form ecclesiastical provinces or larger groupings called patriarchates or regions. The bishops of these groupings can meet in synods or provincial councils. "In a like fashion, the episcopal conferences at the present time are in a position to contribute in many and fruitful ways to the concrete realization of the collegiate spirit."[14]

In these passages from the *Catechism* on the authority of the episcopacy and collegiality we find an ecclesial vision drawn from the teachings of the First Vatican Council, the Second Vatican Council and the experience of the Church in the subsequent forty years of the Post-Vatican II period. We shall now turn to the agreed statement of ARCIC, *The Gift of Authority*, to consider this ecclesial vision in dialogue with the Anglican tradition.

While the *Catechism* is concerned with the relationship between episcopal authority and papal authority, the *Gift of Authority* is concerned with the relationship between episcopal authority and lay authority:

Those who exercise *episcope* in the Body of Christ must not be separated from the "symphony" of the whole people of God in which they have their part to play. They need to be alert to the *sensus fidelium*, which they share, if they are to be made aware when something is needed for the well-being and mission of the community, or when some element of the Tradition needs to be received in a fresh way. The charism and function of *episcope* are specifically connected to the *ministry of memory*, which constantly renews the Church in hope. Through such ministry the Holy Spirit keeps alive in the Church the memory of what God did and revealed, and the hope of what God will do to bring all things into unity in Christ. . . The bishops, the clergy and the other faithful must all recognize and receive what is mediated from God through each other. Thus the *sensus fidelium* of the people of God and the ministry of memory exist together in reciprocal relationship.[15]

The Gift of Authority centers episcopal authority clearly in the context of the communal authority of the faithful of the local Church, emphasizing the reciprocal relationship of co-responsibility that clergy and laity have together for the life of faith and mission of the Church. The authority given by Christ to the community and its leaders is for service and the building up of the Body of Christ:

> The authority which Jesus bestowed on his disciples was, above all, the authority for mission, to preach and to heal. The Risen Christ empowered them to spread the Gospel to the whole world. In the early Church, the preaching of the Word of God in the power of the Spirit was seen as the defining characteristic of apostolic authority. . .Thus, the exercise of ministerial authority within the Church, not least by those entrusted with the ministry of *episcope,* has a radically missionary dimension. Authority is exercised within the Church for the sake of those outside it, that the Gospel may be proclaimed "in power and in the Holy Spirit and will full conviction" (1 Thess 1:5). This authority enables the whole Church to embody the Gospel and become the missionary and prophetic servant of the Lord.[16]

At the beginning of the 21st Century the Church is called to missionary authority and prophetic servant-hood which works for reconciliation in broader society by first re-establishing unity amidst the diverse Christian traditions:

> The challenge and responsibility for those within the Church is to exercise their ministry so that they promote the unity of the whole Church in faith and life in a way that enriches rather than diminishes the legitimate diversity of local churches. In each local church all the faithful are called to walk together in Christ. The term *synodality* (derived from *syn-hodos*) meaning "common way" indicates the manner in which believers and churches are held together in communion as they do this. . .Within the communion of local churches the Spirit is at work to shape each church through the grace of reconciliation and communion in Christ. It is only through the activity of the Spirit that the local church can be faithful to the "Amen" of Christ and can be sent into the world to draw all people to participate in this "Amen." Through this presence of the Spirit the local church is maintained in the Tradition. It receives and shares the fullness of the apostolic faith and the means of grace. The Spirit confirms the local church in the truth in such a way that its life embodies the saving truth revealed in Christ. From generation to generation the authority of the living Word should be made present in the local church through all aspects of its life in the world. The way in which authority is exercised in the structures and corporate life of the Church must be conformed to the mind of Christ. (cf. Phil 2.5).[17]

The mutual exercise of episcopal and lay authority within the local church in the pattern of Christ the servant is a manifestation of the work of the Spirit drawing all into unity amidst diversity. The mutual sharing of gifts by pastors and laity is a powerful witness of unity in diversity that enriches the communion (*koinonia*) of all the local churches. It is also a witness to the reconciliation that is possible by the power of the Spirit:

The Spirit of Christ endows each bishop with the pastoral authority needed for the effective exercise of *episcope* within a local church. This authority neces- sarily includes responsibility for making and implementing the decisions that are required to fulfill the office of a bishop for the sake of *koinonia*. Its binding authority is implicit in the bishop's task of teaching the faith through the procla- mation and explanation of the Word of God, of providing for the celebration of the sacraments, and of maintaining the Church in holiness and truth . . . By their *sensus fidei* the faithful are able in conscience both to recognize God at work in the bishop's exercise of authority, and also to respond to it as believers. . .Within the working of the *sensus fidelium* there is a complementary relationship be- tween the bishop and the rest of the community. In the local church the Eucharist is the fundamental expression of the walking together synodality of the people of God.[18]

Pastors and laity in local churches are bound together by the Eucharist as the source of renewed life in the crucified and risen Lord. The Holy Spirit Who renews local churches in their unity amidst diversity by the Eucharist also draws them through baptism and Eucharist into the communion of all the churches together that it is the body of Christ, the Church:

The mutual interdependence of all the churches is integral to the reality of the Church as God wills it to be. No local church that participates in the living Tra- dition can regard itself as self-sufficient. Forms of synodality, then, are needed to manifest the communion of the local churches and to sustain each of them in fidelity to the Gospel. The ministry of the bishop is crucial, for this ministry serves communion within and among local churches. Their communion with each other is expressed through the incorporation of each bishop into a college of bishops. Bishops are, both personally and collegially, at the service of com- munion and are concerned for synodality in all its expressions. These expres- sions include a variety of organs, instruments and institutions, notably synods or councils, local, provincial, worldwide, ecumenical. The maintenance of com- munion requires that at every level there is a capacity to take decisions appro- priate to that level. When those decisions raise serious questions for the wider communion of churches, synodality must find a wider expression. In both our communions, the bishops meet together collegially, not as individuals but as those who have authority within and for the synodal life of the local churches. Consulting the faithful is an aspect of episcopal oversight. Each bishop is both a voice for the local church and one through whom the local church learns from other churches. When bishops take counsel together they seek both to discern and to articulate the *sensus fidelium* as it is present in the local church and in the wider communion of churches.[19]

The Anglican and Roman Catholic bishops and theologians who worked to- gether to create the agreed statement, the *Gift of Authority,* recognized the

The realization that the structures of ecclesial relationship of the first millennium breathe a spirit of communion that must be regained, but that we cannot try to return to the past is an important horizon for moving forward. As the Anglican bishops indicate, we must be "faithful to the present context and the demands of common life, witness and service today."

The relationship between the Pope and the college of bishops is one of immense importance for the internal life of the Roman Church, for ecumenical dialogues and, as the Anglican Bishops indicate, at this juncture for the question of primacy and collegiality in the Anglican Communion:

> The relationship in both theory and practice between the Pope and the college of bishops is one particular area where we have already indicated a need for further investigation. This is not a purely Roman Catholic question, and many churches are currently discussing the interrelationship between primacy and collegiality. This is the subject of special studies in the Church of England and the Anglican Communion as a whole. It is closely related to another area of concern in modern Anglican ecclesiology, namely the relationship between the responsibilities possessed by a 'Province' for its own affairs and its responsibility towards other Provinces and churches. It is widely recognized that within our Anglican Communion there is a danger that 'provincial autonomy' may be taken to mean 'independence.' Some consider that a primatial ministry with an appropriate collegial and conciliar structure is essential if this danger is to be avoided.[24]

In the dialogue about primacy and conciliarity and the significance of the structures of the first millennium, dialogue with the Orthodox churches is significant for the churches of the West, as the Anglican bishops point out:

> We note that the communion between the Roman Catholic Church and the Orthodox churches is described as almost complete despite the fact that the latter are not in visible communion with the Bishop of Rome. In this context we recall some words of Cardinal Ratzinger: "As far as the doctrine of primacy is concerned, Rome must not require more of the East than was formulated during the first millennium . . . Reunion could take place on this basis: that for its part the East should renounce attacking the western developments of the second millennium as heretical, and should accept the Catholic [sic] Church as legitimate and orthodox in the form which it has found through this development, while for its part, the West should acknowledge the Church of the East as orthodox and legitimate in the form which it has maintained." Such an approach offers considerable hope, and could make possible a fresh consideration of many matters in which churches have developed in separation from one another.[25]

The Roman Catholic and Anglican bishops and theologians of ARCIC II were very conscious of the current Roman Catholic teaching on the primacy of the bishop of Rome, the response of the House of Bishops of the Church of England, and the agreed statements, *Authority in the Church I* and *Authority in the Church II* formulated by ARCIC I, as they returned to the consideration of primacy in *The Gift of Authority:*

> ARCIC has already recognized that the "pattern of complementary primatial and conciliar aspects of *episcope* serving the *koinonia* of the churches needs to be realized at the universal level" (*Authority in the Church I*, 23). The exigencies of church life call for a specific exercise of *episcope* at the service of the whole Church. In the pattern found in the New Testament one of the twelve is chosen by Jesus Christ to strengthen the others so that they will remain faithful to their mission and in harmony with each other (see the discussion of the Petrine texts in *Authority in the Church II*, 2–5). Augustine of Hippo expressed well the relationship among Peter, the other apostles and the whole Church, when he said: "After all, it is not just one man that received these keys, but the Church in its unity. So this is the reason for Peter's acknowledged preeminence, that he stood for the Church's universality and unity, when he was told, *to You I am entrusting*, what has in fact been entrusted to all. I mean to show you that it is the Church which has received the keys of the kingdom of heaven. Listen to what the Lord says in another place to all his apostles: *Receive the Holy Spirit, and straight away whose sins you forgive, they will be forgiven them; whose sins you retain, they will be retained* (John 20:22–23). This refers to the keys, about which is said, *whatever you bind on earth shall be bound in heaven* (Mt. 16.19). But that was said to Peter . . . Peter at that time stood for the universal Church" (*Sermon 295, On the Feast of the Martyrdom of the Apostles Peter and Paul*). ARCIC has also previously explored the transmission of the primatial ministry exercised by the Bishop of Rome (see *Authority in the Church II*, 6–9). Historically, the Bishop of Rome has exercised such a ministry either for the benefit of the whole church, as when Leo contributed to the Council of Chalcedon, or for the benefit of a local church, as when Gregory the Great supported Augustine of Canterbury's mission and ordering of the English Church. This gift has been welcomed and the ministry of these Bishops of Rome continues to be celebrated liturgically by Anglicans as well as Roman Catholics.[26]

The bishops and theologians responsible for *The Gift of Authority* also wanted us to be conscious of human fragility and the constant need for conversion that are also a significant dimension of the exercise of authority in the Church:

> It is clear that only by the grace of God does the exercise of authority in the communion of the Church bear the marks of Christ's own authority. This authority is exercised by fragile Christians for the sake of other fragile Christians. This is no less true of the ministry of Peter: "Simon, Simon, listen! Satan has demanded to sift all of you like wheat, but I have prayed for you that your own faith may

not fail; and you, when once you have turned back, strengthen your brothers"
(Lk 22:32–32). Pope John Paul II makes this clear in *Ut Unum Sint:* "I carry out
this duty with the profound conviction that I am obeying the Lord, and with a
clear sense of my own frailty. Indeed, if Christ Himself gave Peter this special
mission in the Church and exhorted him to strengthen his brethren, He also
made clear to him his human weakness, and his special need of conversion" (*Ut
Unum Sint*, 4). Human weakness and sin do not only affect individual ministers:
they can distort the human structuring of authority (Cf Mt. 23). Therefore, loyal
criticism and reforms are sometimes needed, following the example of Paul (cf
Gal 2:11–14). The consciousness of human frailty in the exercise of authority
ensures that Christian ministers remain open to criticism and renewal and above
all to exercising authority according to the example and mind of Christ.[27]

The 1981 agreed statement, *Authority in the Church II,* expresses very
clearly an ecumenical vision for exercising the authority of universal primacy,
which is at the service of unity amidst diversity:

> If primacy is to be a genuine expression of *episcope* it will foster the *koinonia*
> by helping the bishops in their task of apostolic leadership both in their local
> church and in the Church universal. Primacy fulfills its purpose by helping the
> churches to listen to one another, to grow in love and unity, and to strive together
> towards the fullness of Christian life and witness; it respects and promotes
> Christian freedom and spontaneity; it does not seek uniformity where diversity
> is legitimate, or centralize administration to the detriment of local churches. A
> primate exercises his ministry not in isolation but in collegial association with
> his brother bishops. His intervention in the affairs of a local church should not
> be made in such a way as to usurp the responsibility of its bishop.[28]

The ecumenical perspective which this understanding of primacy presents is
indicative of what the Bishops of the Church of England call an "ecumenical
methodology," that is to say one which "willingly leaves behind the language
of past polemics in the search for a common understanding in faith."[29] The
pastoral existentialist approach to primacy of ARCIC stands in marked contrast to the juridical essentialist approach to papal primacy presented in *The
Catechism*. If the words of Pope John Paul II in *Ut Unum Sint*—"I am convinced that I have a particular responsibility . . .in heeding the request made
of me to find a way of exercising the primacy which, while in no way renouncing what is essential to its mission, is nonetheless open to an new situation"[30]—are to be realized, there does indeed need to be a profound *kenosis*
that lets go of the current mode of understanding and exercising papal primacy. That *kenosis* calls for a re-reception of the authentic apostolic Tradition
of the Petrine office of the first millennium and a letting go of traditions of
the Petrine office of the second millennium that are often in conflict with the

Gospel understanding of authority as service to unity amidst diversity. Although the *Catechism* carefully distinguishes between Apostolic Tradition and subsequent theological, disciplinary, liturgical and devotional traditions, and indicates that the latter can be retained, modified or abandoned under the guidance of the Church's magisterium,[31] that distinction has not always been observed in practice. Ways of structuring the exercise of papal jurisdiction that represent traditions that are now hindrances to Christian unity need to be rectified in light of the penumatic correctives that the Holy Spirit is providing through the ecumencial dialogues between the Roman Catholic Church and other Christian Churches.

The institutional conversion to which the bishop of Rome as the successor of Peter is being called is a return to the New Testament understanding of Peter as disciple, apostle and martyr and not the second millennium understanding of Peter as the Vicar of Christ, the Supreme Pontiff of the Universal Church and the Sovereign of Vatican City State. We need to see the bishop of Rome once more as the servant of the servants of God and not an absolute monarch. We cannot expect other Christians to accept the ecclesiology of Vatican I, which describes the Pope as having full, supreme and universal power over the whole Church, which he can always exercise unhindered, when there is no truly convincing basis for this assertion in the apostolic Tradition. This second millennium understanding of the papacy cannot be essential when there is no evidence that the undivided Church of the first millennium understood the role of the bishop of Rome in this way, as the Churches of the East clearly point out to us.

In recognizing its own responsibilities for the current disunity of Christians, it is not sufficient for the Roman Catholic Church to acknowledge that there were unworthy popes. We must also acknowledge that structures of Papal governance and modes of exercising the Petrine office during the second millennium, although explainable in terms of the culture of the time, were nevertheless often contrary to the New Testament understanding of authority as walking in the footsteps of Christ, who came to serve and not to be served. The quantum leaps of Nicholas I, Gregory VII, Innocent III and Boniface VIII in understanding the nature and extent of Papal power, which we discussed in Chapter 5, have no sound basis in the apostolic Tradition and created a mindset from which we must now disengage ourselves for the sake of the unity of the Church and its mission of preaching the Gospel in the complex world of the 21st century.

The *kenosis* to which the Holy Spirit is calling the bishop of Rome for the sake of Christian unity and mission is an invitation to enter anew into the mystery of Peter, disciple, apostle and martyr, as he served the unity amidst diversity of the apostolic Church. When we look at the Petrine ministry in the

New Testament, we must be attentive not only to what is said, but also to what is not said. In the *Acts of the Apostles* there is no mention of Peter going to Rome, as there is for Paul, and there is no mention of Peter's ministry in Rome, as there is for Paul. Neither is there any mention of Peter appointing a successor to himself or to his disciples, as is the case with Paul and his disciples, Timothy and Titus. The Apostolic Tradition focuses its emphasis on the death of Peter in Rome as a martyr laying down his life for his flock, which is reflected in Chapters 20 and 21 of John's Gospel. The absence of any clear mention of Peter exercising a ministry in Rome in the New Testament serves as a pneumatic corrective to prevent any interpretation that would associate his ministry of service with an exercise of authority that reflected the worldly authority of the Roman Emperors. Rather, he exercised true apostolic authority by witnessing to the resurrection, laying down his life as a martyr in the pattern of Christ the servant. The ministry of Peter described in *Acts* 1–12 is always in concert with the other apostles. At the end of Chapter 12 Peter yields the leadership of the Church to James, the brother of the Lord, and becomes an itinerant missionary. There is no suggestion that Peter ever exercised authority over the whole Church after he left Jerusalem or that he later did so from Rome. The New Testament does not portray Peter as a universal monarch of the Church, but as the servant leader who guides the community at Jerusalem in communal witness and service. When Peter fails to live up to his pastoral obligations at Antioch, he is rightly corrected by Paul, reminding us that the exercise of the Petrine ministry needs the complementarity of the Pauline ministry as a corrective. Re-reception of the mystery of Peter, as it is presented in the Apostolic Tradition, by the bishops of Rome of the 21st century would lead us toward the recovery of the universal primacy envisioned by the agreed statement, *Authority II,* when it speaks of a primacy that helps churches listen to one another, to grow in love and unity and to strive for the fullness of Christian witness because it respects the freedom of local churches. It does not seek uniformity where diversity is legitimate and does not centralize administration to the detriment of local churches.

Eusebius of Caesarea gives us a wonderful example from the Early Church of the interaction of Petrine and Pauline ministry in his *History of the Church*. Amidst the second century controversy over the date of Easter between the churches of Asia Minor and the church of Rome, Irenaeus of Lyons wrote to Victor of Rome urging him not to try to force the Eastern churches to conform to the Roman pattern. In his letter that served as a Pauline corrective from the bishop of Lyons to the bishop of Rome, he brought forward the example of Victor's predecessor Ancietus, who had being willing to be the servant of unity amidst diversity when Polycarp of Symrna came to Rome for a visit:

And when Blessed Polycarp paid a visit to Rome in Anicetus' time, though they had minor differences on other matters too, they at once made peace, having no desire to quarrel on this point, Anicetus could not persuade Polycarp not to keep the day, since he had always kept in with John the disciple of our Lord and the other apostles with whom he had been familiar; nor did Polycarp persuade Anicetus to keep it: Anicetus said that he must stick to the practice of the presbyters before him. Though the position was such, they remained in communion with each other, and in church Anicetus made way for Polycarp to celebrate the Eucharist—out of respect obviously. They parted company in peace, and the whole Church was at peace, both those who kept the day and those who did not.[32]

As we seek to find new ways to harmonize the authority of primacy and conciliarity, Anicetus and Polycarp are wonderful models of the bishop of Rome and the bishop of Symrna exercising *episcope* together for the sake of *koinonia,* and Anicetus yielding the presiding role at Eucharist to Polycarp is a wonderful symbol of the bishop of Rome exercising the Petrine ministry by living the reality of unity amidst diversity.

TEACHING AUTHORITY

The *Catechism* provides the Roman Catholic Church's vision of teaching authority within the Church:

In order to preserve the Church in the purity of the faith handed on by the apostles, Christ who is the Truth willed to confer on her a share in his own infallibility. By a "supernatural sense of faith" the People of God, under the guidance of the Church's living Magisterium, "unfailingly adheres to this faith." The mission of the Magisterium is linked to the definitive nature of the covenant established by God with his people in Christ. It is this Magisterium's task to preserve God's people from deviations and defections and to guarantee them the objective possibility of professing the true faith without error. Thus, the pastoral duty of the Magisterium is aimed at seeing that the People of God abides in the truth that liberates. To fulfill this service, Christ endowed the Church's shepherds with the charism of infallibility in matters of faith and morals. The exercise of this charism takes several forms: "The Roman Pontiff, head of the college of bishops, enjoys this infallibility in virtue of his office, when, as supreme pastor and teacher of all the faithful—who confirms his brethren in the faith—he proclaims by a definitive act a doctrine pertaining to faith or morals. . .The infallibility promised to the Church is also present in the body of bishops when, together with Peter's successor, they exercise the supreme Magisterium," above all in an Ecumenical Council. When the Church through its supreme Magisterium proposes a doctrine "for belief as being divinely revealed," and as the teaching of Christ, the definitions "must be adhered to with the obedience of faith." This infallibility extends as far as the deposit of divine Revelation itself. Divine Assistance is also given to the successors of the apostles, teaching in communion with the successor of Peter, and, in a particular way, to the bishop of Rome, pastor of the whole Church, when, without arriving at an infallible definition and without pronouncing in a "definitive manner," they propose in the exercise of the ordinary Magisterium a teaching that leads to better understanding of Revelation in matters of faith and morals. To this ordinary teaching the faithful "are to adhere to it with religious assent" which, though distinct from the assent of faith, is nonetheless an extension of it.[33]

From an ecumenical perspective, the Roman Catholic understanding of teaching authority presents a number of challenging issues, which *The Gift of Authority* seeks to address:

In its continuing life, the Church seeks and receives the guidance from the Holy Spirit that keeps its teachings faithful to apostolic Tradition. Within the whole body, the college of bishops is to exercise the ministry of memory to this end. They are to discern and give teaching which may be trusted because it expresses the truth of God surely. In some situations, there will be an urgent need to test new formulations of faith. In specific circumstances, those with this ministry of oversight (*episcope*), assisted by the Holy Spirit, may together come to a judgement which, being faithful to Scripture and consistent with apostolic Tradition, is preserved from error. By such a judgment, which is a renewed expression of God's one "yes" in Jesus Christ, the Church is maintained in the truth so that it may continue to offer its "Amen" to the glory of God. This is what is meant when it is affirmed that the Church may teach *infallibly* . . . Such infallible teaching is at the service of the Church's indefectibility. The exercise of teaching authority in the Church, especially in situations of challenge, requires the participation, in their distinctive ways, of the whole body of believers, not only those charged with the ministry of memory. In this participation the *sensus fidelium* is at work. Since it is the faithfulness of the whole people that is at stake, reception of teaching is integral to the process. Doctrinal definitions are received as authoritative in virtue of the divine truth they proclaim as well as because of the specific office of the person or persons who proclaim them within the *sensus fidei* of the whole people of God. When the people of God respond by faith and say "Amen" to authoritative teaching it is because they recognize that this teaching expresses the apostolic faith and operates within the authority and truth of Christ, the Head of the Church . . . The duty of maintaining the Church in the truth is one of the essential functions of the episcopal college. It has the power to exercise this ministry because it is bound in succession to the apostles, who were the body authorized and sent by Christ to preach the Gospel to all the nations. The authenticity of the teaching of individual bishops is evident when this teaching is in solidarity with that of the whole episcopal college. The exercise of this teaching authority requires that what it teaches be faithful

to Holy Scripture and consistent with the apostolic Tradition. This is expressed
by the teaching of the Second Vatican Council, "This teaching office is not
above the Word of God, but serves it" (Dogmatic Constitution on Divine Revelation, *Dei Verbum, 10).*[34]

Having presented an overall understanding of teaching authority, *The Gift
of Authority* then proceeds to address the ministry of the Bishop of Rome as
teacher and the issue of infallibility:

> Within his wider ministry, the Bishop of Rome offers a specific ministry con-
> cerning the discernment of truth, as an expression of universal primacy. This
> particular service has been the source of difficulties and misunderstandings
> among the churches. Every solemn definition pronounced from the chair of Pe-
> ter in the church of Peter and Paul may, however, express only the faith of the
> Church. Any such definition is pronounced *within* the college of those who ex-
> ercise *episcope* and not outside that college. Such authoritative teaching is a par-
> ticular exercise of the calling and responsibility of the body of bishops to teach
> and affirm the faith. When the faith is articulated in this way, the Bishop of
> Rome proclaims the faith of the local churches. It is thus the wholly reliable
> teaching of the whole Church that is operative in the judgment of the universal
> primate. In solemnly formulating such teaching, the universal primate must dis-
> cern and declare, with the assured assistance and guidance of the Holy Spirit, in
> fidelity to Scripture and Tradition, the authentic faith of the whole Church, that
> is, the faith proclaimed from the beginning. It is this faith, the faith of all the
> baptized in communion, and this only, that each bishop utters with the body of
> bishops in council. It is this faith which the Bishop of Rome in certain circum-
> stances has a duty to discern and make explicit. This form of authoritative teach-
> ing has no stronger guarantee from the Spirit than have the solemn definitions
> of ecumenical councils. The reception of the primacy of the Bishop of Rome en-
> tails the recognition of this specific ministry of the universal primate. We be-
> lieve that this is a gift to be received by all the churches.[35]

The issue of teaching authority in the Church is related to the issue of primacy. What we said in terms of ecumenical methodology in relation to primacy is also true of teaching authority. The essentialist approach of *The Catechism* stands in marked contrast to the existentialist approach of *The Gift of
Authority.* The central focus of teaching authority for *The Catechism* is the
Bishop of Rome, while *The Gift of Authority* looks to the whole of the Christian community with its diverse charisms that together hand on and preserve
the Apostolic Tradition. The Roman Catholic Church has still not tempered
the one-sided vision of authority focused on the papacy that emerged from the
First Vatican Council. Although the Second Vatican Council tried to rectify
this situation through its teachings on episcopal collegiality and teaching
authority, the Roman Catholic Church remains locked into a 19th century

understanding of the role of the Bishop of Rome and an unbalanced view of ecclesial teaching authority. The ecumenical dialogues of the 20th century with the Eastern Orthodox, Anglican and Lutheran traditions, who have preserved episcopacy as a focus for the ministry of memory of the Apostolic Tradition, have served as a pneumatic corrective for the continuing over emphasis of the Roman tradition on the teaching authority of the Bishop of Rome to the detriment of the other teaching authorities integral to the fullness of the Christian tradition.

Gift of Authority, while acknowledging the positive role that the Bishop of Rome has in helping to maintain the Church's fidelity to the Apostolic Tradition, also recognizes that under the guidance of the Holy Spirit this ministry of memory of the Bishop of Rome must be joined to that of the bishops of the universal Church and to the *sensus fidei* of the people of God as a whole. The world-wide community of theologians with diverse theological perspectives also has a crucial role to play in the formulation of teaching that is truly faithful to the Apostolic Tradition and is not merely the outlook of one of the theological schools of a particular place and time. The theologians who served as *periti* to the bishops of the Second Vatican Council exemplify the kind of mutual co-operation between pastors and theologians that seeks to preserve the Apostolic Tradition while formulating the faith in meaningful ways for new generations of Christians. We also need to find ways in which the prophetic function of clergy and laity, who may or may not be theologians, can find expression so that the *sensus fidei* given to them by the Holy Spirit can find its rightful place in handing on the Apostolic Tradition. As *The Gift of Authority* indicates, reception of new formulations of the Apostolic Tradition by the people of God is an integral part of the teaching mission shared by all the members of the Church, who have been endowed at baptism with the gift of the Holy Spirit and find that gift ever renewed in the celebration of the Eucharist. The Holy Spirit as teacher is present in all baptized Christians, not only the pastors and theologians of the Church. The pastors of the Church need to be more deeply aware of the *sensus fidei* of the People of God and respect their baptismal right to share in the teaching authority of the Church.

The traditional understanding of the Church in the East and the West is that the supreme exercise of teaching authority, Magisterium, is in an Ecumenical Council. The New Testament paradigm for this understanding is the Council of Jerusalem in *Acts of the Apostles* 15, where the apostles and the elders with Peter, James the head of the Jerusalem Church, Paul and Barnabas and members of the community gathered to decide to what extent Gentile Christians would be bound by the prescriptions of the Mosaic law. In communicating to the Gentile Christian communities they said: "It is the decision of the Holy Spirit and of us not to place any burden beyond these necessities, namely to abstain from meat sacrificed to idols, from blood, from meats of strangled animals, and from un-lawful marriage" (*Acts* 15: 28–29). The text makes clear the belief of the apos-tolic Church that a gathering representing the whole Church was empowered by the Holy Spirit to make decisions which made continuity with the apostolic faith possible in new situations. In the Pre-Constantinian Church, gatherings of bish-ops, representing local churches, in regional or provincial synods to discuss mat-ters of doctrine and discipline became common in the second and third centuries. In the Constantinian and Post-Constantinian Church of the Christian Roman Empire, the Emperors called Ecumenical Councils representing the whole Church to decide crucial issues pertaining to doctrine and practice. The Bishop of Rome was not present at any of the seven great Ecumenical Councils of the first millennium, which articulated the Apostolic Tradition anew in the Trinitar-ian and Christological formulations that guide the Churches of East and West to the present time, but he was represented by his legates and subsequently ap-proved the conciliar decisions totally or partially. For the Churches of the East and for Protestant Christians of the West the seven great Councils of the first mil-lennium are the only truly Ecumenical Councils, while for Catholic Christians thirteen subsequent councils held in the West during the second millennium from Lateran I (1123) to Vatican II (1962–1965) are also considered Ecumenical Councils.

For the sake of Christian unity the Roman Catholic Church is being called to the *kenosis* of acknowledging that the thirteen councils of the Western Church from 1123 to 1962–1965 are not truly ecumenical councils because they did not represent the whole Church. Hence their decisions are not per-petually binding and could be modified or changed by a future Ecumenical Council that did represent the one, holy, catholic and apostolic church. The Council of Constance (1414–1418), which ended the great western schism, mandated that general councils be held every 10 years for the continual re-form and renewal of the Church. Had the Renaissance popes of the fifteenth and early sixteenth centuries implemented this conciliar decision, the Refor-mation that divided western Christendom might have been averted.

As the Lambeth Conferences of the Anglican Communion meets every ten years under the presidency of the Archbishop of Canterbury, so, too, Ecu-menical Councils of different Christian traditions of the East and West bound together in ecclesial communion could meet together every ten years under the presidency of the Bishop of Rome. Delegates to such an Ecumenical Council could be chosen from local churches so that pastors and laity could be equally heard and equally participative with the aid of theologians in for-mulating the truths of the faith to meet the diverse catechetical needs of the 21st century. At the heart of the work of Ecumenical Councils would be the preservation of unity amidst diversity of the Apostolic Tradition.

CONCLUSION

Pope John Paul's desire to find a way of exercising papal primacy that does not renounce what is essential to its mission, but is open to a new situation, is a formidable challenge to the Roman Catholic Church. At the heart of the problem is discerning what is and is not essential to its mission. From an essentialist perspective, such as that manifest in *The Catechism,* whatever is now present in the current understanding and functioning of the ministry of the Bishop of Rome is essential, while from an existentialist perspective, such as that present in *The Gift of Authority,* much could be changed while still maintaining what truly is essential to the universal ministry of the Bishop of Rome as the servant of unity in diversity. Those who serve the Bishop of Rome in various capacities in the Roman Curia take very seriously their responsibility to preserve the full integrity of the Apostolic Tradition. The ethos of the guardians of the faith of the Roman Catholic Church, however, may create an environment in which any real change is seen as unacceptable. It is not always easy to distinguish the Apostolic Tradition from the ecclesial traditions of the past and to be willing to let go of traditions no longer helpful to the life and mission of the Church. The Roman Catholic and Anglican bishops and theologians who wrote *The Gift of Authority* sought carefully to find a *via media* that preserved the Apostolic Tradition but also recognized the need to re-examine the ecclesial traditions. We are at a crucial juncture in the search for Christian unity. We need the Bishop of Rome to enter anew into the *kenotic* mystery of the ministry of Peter, disciple, apostle and martyr so that he can find the grace of the Holy Spirit to lead us forward on the path of reform and renewal.

NOTES

1. *Catechism of the Catholic Church* (Second Edition), (Washington, D.C.: United States Catholic Conference, 2000), 24–25.

2. *Catechism*, 26–27.

3. Anglican-Roman Catholic International Commission (ARCIC), *The Gift of Authority: Authority in the Church III* (New York, NY: Church Publishing Incorporated, 1999), 17.

4. ARCIC, *Gift of Authority,* 18.

5. *Catechism*, 237.

6. *Catechism*, 238.

7. *Catechism*, 239–240.

8. *Catechism,* 240.

9. ARCIC, *Gift of Authority*, 21.

10. ARCIC, *Gift of Authority*, 21–22.

11. ARCIC, *Gift of Authority*, 23.

12. *Catechism*, 233–234.

13. *Catechism*, 234.

14. *Catechism*, 234–235.

15. ARCIC, *Gift of Authority*, 24.

16. ARCIC, *Gift of Authority*, 25.

17. ARCIC, *Gift of Authority*, 26–27.

18. ARCIC, *Gift of Authority*, 27.

19. ARCIC, *Gift of Authority*, 27–28.

20. *Catechism*, 234.

21. The House of Bishops of the Church of England (HBCE), *May They All Be One: A Response to Ut Unum Sint* (London: Church House Publishing, 1997), 17.

22. HBCE, *May They All Be One*, 18.

23. HBCE, *May They All Be One*, 19.

24. HBCE, *May They All Be One*, 19–20.

25. HBCE, *May They All Be One*, 20.

26. ARCIC, *Gift of Authority*, 32–33.

27. ARCIC, *Gift of Authority*, 34–35.

28. ARCIC, *Gift of Authority*, 51.

29. HBCE, *May They All Be One*, 6.

30. Pope John Paul II, "Ut Unum Sint," *Origins*, 25:4 (Spring 1995): 69.

31. *Catechism*, 26–27.

32. Eusebius, *The History of the Church from Christ to Constantine*, in trans. G.A. Williamson (New York: Dorset Press, 1984), 233 (5:24:13).

33. *Catechism*, 235–236.

34. ARCIC, *Gift of Authority*, 31–32.

35. ARCIC, *Gift of Authority*, 33–34.

Index

Made in the USA
Lexington, KY
07 January 2013